RIO GRANDE BLANKETS

Late Nineteenth-Century Textiles in Transition

BY KELLEN KEE MCINTYRE

Introduction by Marian Rodee

adobe gallery
art of the southwest indian

© 1992 Adobe Gallery
413 Romero N.W.
Albuquerque, NM 87104
(505) 243-8485

Library of Congress Cataloging-in-Publication Data

McIntyre, Kellen Kee.
    Rio Grande blankets: late nineteenth-century textiles in transition / by Kellen Kee McIntyre.
        p.   cm.
    Includes bibliographical references and index.
    1. Blankets--New Mexico--Rio Grande Valley.
2. Textile fabrics--New Mexico--Rio Grande Valley--History--19th century. 3. Sarapes--Influence.
I.Title.
NK8910.N62R565
746.1'4'09789609034--dc20   92-19989
                                        CIP

ISBN 0-9633710-0-2

All rights reserved. No portion of this publication may
be reproduced or transmitted in any form or by any means,
electronic or mechanical, including photocopying,
recording, or any information storage or retrieval system
without permission in writing from the publisher.

*For Winnie M. Pfingsten,
my Aunt "Minnie."*

BLANKETS

1 Classic Rio Grande Five-Band Blanket 44
1 Classic Rio Grande Five-Band Blanket, *detail* 44
2 Transitional Rio Grande Striped Blanket 45
2 Transitional Rio Grande Striped Blanket, *detail* 45
3 Transitional Rio Grande Five-Band Blanket 46
4 Transitional Rio Grande Band and Stripe Blanket 47
4 Transitional Rio Grande Band and Stripe Blanket, *detail* 47
5 Transitional Rio Grande Five-Band Blanket 48
6 Transitional Rio Grande Five-Band Blanket 49
7 Transitional Rio Grande Striped Blanket 50
8 Transitional Rio Grande Striped Blanket 51
8 Transitional Rio Grande Striped Blanket, *detail* 51
9 Transitional Rio Grande Five-Band Blanket 52
10 Transitional Rio Grande Striped Blanket 53
11 Transitional Rio Grande Striped Blanket 54
12 Transitional Rio Grande Striped Blanket 55
13 Transitional Rio Grande Nine-Band Blanket 56
14 Transitional Rio Grande Five-Band Blanket 57
15 Transitional Rio Grande Band and Stripe Blanket 58
16 Transitional Rio Grande Five-Band Blanket 59
17 Transitional Rio Grande Striped Blanket 60
18 Transitional Rio Grande Striped Blanket 61
19 Transitional Rio Grande Six-Band Blanket 62
20 Transitional Rio Grande Seven-Band Blanket with Saltillo Design Elements 63
21 Transitional Rio Grande Saltillo-Style Sampler 64
22 Transitional Rio Grande Saltillo-Style Blanket 65
22 Transitional Rio Grande Saltillo-Style Blanket, *detail* 65
23 Revival Saltillo-Style Blanket 66
24 Early Chimayo Furniture Scarf 67
25 Early Chimayo Blanket 68
25 Early Chimayo Blanket, *detail* 68
26 Modern Chimayo Furniture or Floor Throw 69
26 Modern Chimayo Furniture or Floor Throw, *detail* 69
27 Revival Striped Blanket 70
27 Revival Striped Blanket, *detail* 70
28 Classic Rio Grande Five-Band Blanket 71
29 Saltillo *Sarape* 71
30 Rio Grande Saltillo-Style Blanket (without border) 72
31 Rio Grande Saltillo-Style Blanket (with selvage bands) 72
32 Rio Grande Saltillo-Style Blanket (with frame) 73
33 Rio Grande Seven-Band Blanket with Saltillo Design Elements 73

Unless otherwise noted in the Figure, all photographs in this study are by Studio 7 / Albuquerque.

ILLUSTRATIONS

1 Map of New Mexico 6
   Illustration by Moira North
2 Mexican Loom, Tertio-Mellennial Exposition 37
   Santa Fe, New Mexico, ca. 1883.
   Photo by Ben Wittick
   Courtesy School of American Research Collections
   in the Museum of New Mexico
   Neg. No. 15624
3 Sheep in Sandia or Manzano Mountain Pasture 38
   ca. 1895.
   Albuquerque Museum Photoarchives,
   Van Deren Coke Collection
4 Indian Room, Interior, Alvarado Hotel. 39
   Albuquerque, New Mexico, ca. 1905.
   Courtesy Museum of New Mexico
   Neg. No. 14575
5 Interior Kate Mueller residence. 39
   De Vargas Street, Santa Fe, New Mexico, ca. 1912.
   Photo by Jesse L. Nusbaum.
   Courtesy Museum of New Mexico
   Neg. No. 40924
6 Spanish weaving, carding and spinning. 39
   The Native Market, Santa Fe, New Mexico, ca. 1935.
   Photo by T. Harmon Parkhurst.
   Courtesy Museum of New Mexico
   Neg. No. 145821
7 Store window display. Moore's Men Shop 38
   San Francisco Street, Santa Fe, New Mexico,
   ca. 1935.
   Photo by T. Harmon Parkhurst.
   Courtesy Museum of New Mexico,
   Neg. No. 51553
8 Woman weaving rag rug at WPA Project. 39
   Costilla, New Mexico, September 1939.
   Photo by Russell Lee.
   Courtesy Museum of New Mexico
   Neg. No. 9177
9 Color Frequency Chart 70

CONTENTS

INTRODUCTION 7

HISTORIC MAP OF NEW MEXICO 8

FOREWORD 9

ACKNOWLEDGMENTS 11

PART ONE:
1. RIO GRANDE WEAVING: A CONCISE HISTORY **15**
2. IMPACT OF THE RAILROAD AND THE EARLY COLLECTORS **23**
3. MODERN CRITICISM AND SCHOLARSHIP **29**
4. THE TRANSITIONAL PERIOD RIO GRANDE BLANKET **33**
5. HISTORIC PHOTOGRAPHS **37**

PART TWO:
1. INTRODUCTION TO THE CATALOGUE **42**
2. THE CATALOGUE **43**

APPENDICES
A. COMPARATIVE MATERIALS **71**
B. COLOR FREQUENCY CHART **74**

ENDNOTES 77

REFERENCES CITED 81

GLOSSARY 83

ABBREVIATIONS 83

INDEX 84

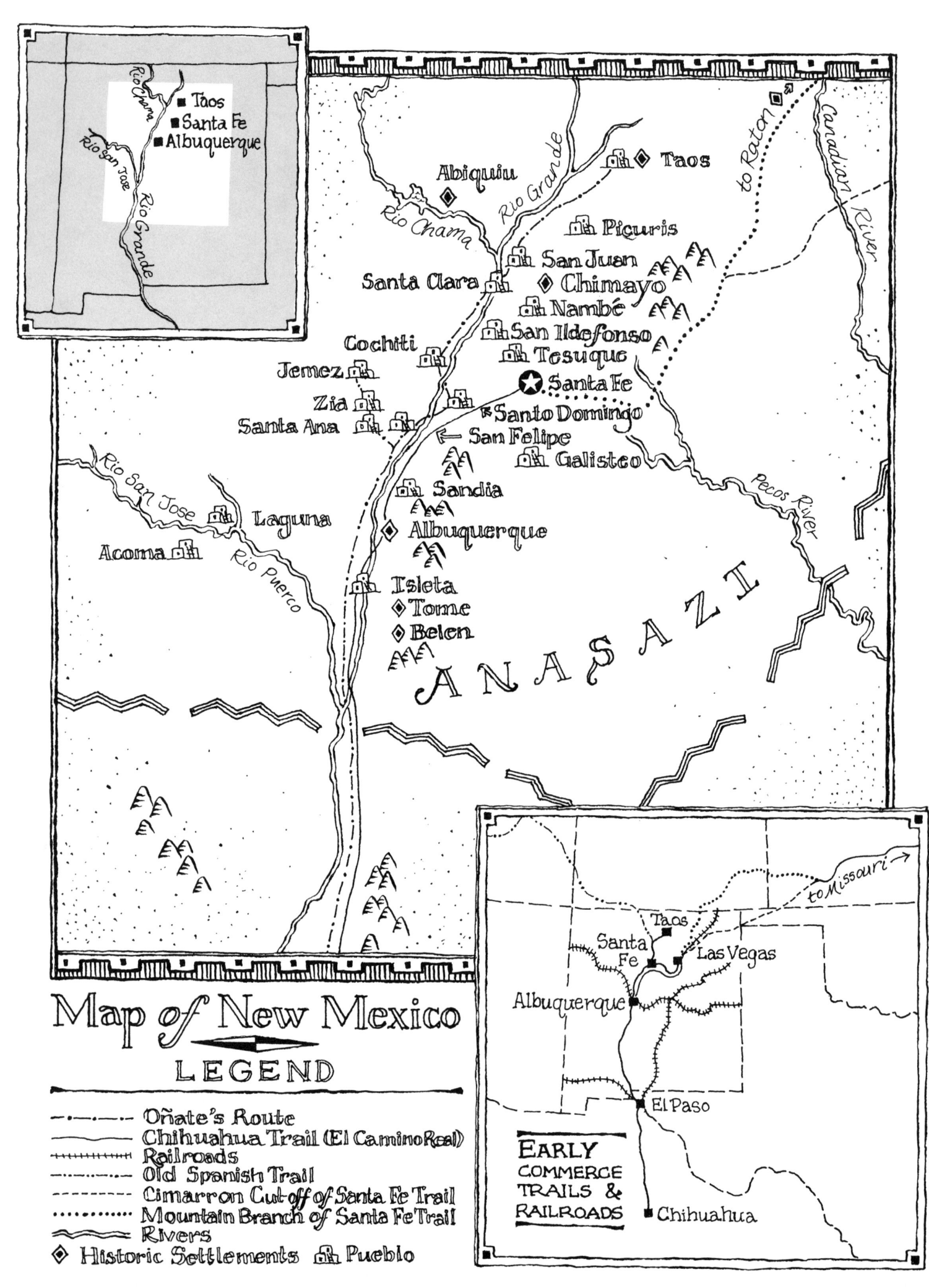

INTRODUCTION

Some Comments on Stripes

BY MARIAN RODEE

STRIPED TEXTILES have a long history in the American Southwest. It has long been a common assumption that cultures begin by weaving simpler patterns, such as stripes, in their textiles and then over time culturally develop more complex and intricate designs. This does not seem to be the case with indigenous cultures in the Southwest, and indeed, this assumption cannot be substantiated. The earliest examples of weaving, including sandals, baskets and other off-the-loom pieces, usually have very angular designs which incorporate meanders or stepped frets. These often elaborate patterns, many polychrome, can also be found on prehistoric pottery, but because so little prehistoric textile material has survived, it is difficult to make any absolute statements about the earliest striped examples.

Navajo blankets from the nineteenth century often employ other patterns superimposed on the stripes; this type of design is most prominently seen at the blanket's corners and center. Frequently in these blankets narrow stripes merely become background filler for the large overlaid design. However, in nineteenth-century Rio Grande blankets, stripes are not used in the same way as those found in Navajo blankets. Perhaps this is because of the different functions of textiles in the two cultures. Navajo textiles were primarily used for saddle blankets and clothing. Thus, a saddle blanket would naturally emphasize the four corners of the textile that project from beneath the saddle. In much the same way, a blanket made to be wrapped around the human body would put a design down the middle of the back of the wearer. While Rio Grande blankets were often worn, their function was much more diverse — rugs, bedding and sacking — enabling Rio Grande blankets to have a broader domestic presence.

The most famous of Navajo striped patterns, the "Chief's Blanket," was the favorite style for trade among Plains Indian people. This is evidenced both in the actual textiles preserved in museums as belonging to the Sioux, Cheyenne and Utes, and also in early photographs and paintings that ethnographically illustrate the clothing worn by these Native Americans. Before the influence of the intricate Rio Grande Saltillo style, the earliest known Chief's Blanket patterns employed wide, visually dynamic horizontal bands. The popularity enjoyed by these blankets among the Northern Plains people mirrors a similar preference for the striped machine-made Hudson's Bay blanket, which was available through Anglo trade.

While stripes may appear to the viewer to be the simplest of all textile patterns, they are really surprisingly difficult to weave, and especially to do so well. Weavers with a long ancestral tradition understand the degree of mental planning that goes into each textile. Smooth and crisp, the striped pattern must visually create a syncopated rhythm to the eye. Today, young Navajo girls learn to make small striped samplers on miniature looms, reminders of the living tradition of which they are a part.

FOREWORD

THE TWENTY-SEVEN BLANKETS reproduced and analyzed in this book were woven by Hispanic weavers in New Mexico from the mid-nineteenth century to about 1940.[1] Because many of these weavers lived in the Rio Grande Valley, textiles produced by them are called "Rio Grande blankets."

The term "Rio Grande blanket" was coined by H. P. Mera in 1910. He used it to refer to all Hispanic weaving in New Mexico dating from the early decades of the twentieth century.[2] The Spanish had colonized the area along the Rio Grande from the Rio Abajo in Central New Mexico to the Rio Arriba in Northern New Mexico. In the mid-1800s Hispanic colonization spread into the San Luis Valley in Southern Colorado.

The Rio Grande blanket had great cultural and economic importance throughout the history of its production. Produced in the home, for the most part, it represented a total family effort, from sheep raising and wool gathering, to yarn production, weaving and actual use. Special blankets were handed down from generation to generation, revered as important family heirlooms and as teaching examples for future family weavers.

Throughout much of the period of its production, the Rio Grande blanket was a major export good. It was used as a trade item for staples and luxuries not readily available in provincial New Mexico. As the quality and variety of Rio Grande blankets increased in the early decades of the 1800s, they became even more sought after, first as an export to Mexico, and later to the United States.

Cultural changes took place in the 1800s due to an increasing American presence. Slowly at first with the opening of the Santa Fe Trail in 1821, and then more rapidly after the 1850s with the opening of the territory and the arrival of the American military, these influences were reflected in the physical characteristics of the Rio Grande blanket itself.

With the arrival of the railroad to New Mexico in 1879-80, imported inexpensive, time-saving goods, such as synthetic dyes and commercial yarns, previously available in only limited quantities, flooded the local market. American influences were so strong and affected the Rio Grande blanket to such a degree that mid-1900s Southwestern scholars scarcely recognized it as a continuation of the Rio Grande tradition. Only recently these late Rio Grande blankets, referred to as "transitional," have begun to be appreciated. Because of early scholarly prejudice and a lack of pertinent data, they were often overlooked and viewed as second-rate. The situation may be likened to that of the post-classic Navajo textiles from the same period, now collected and studied as the prized "Navajo Eyedazzlers."

Part One presents a concise history of the Rio Grande blanket, from Coronado's *entrada* into New Mexico (1540) to the arrival of the railroad in 1879-80. This is followed by an analysis of how the Rio Grande blanket was viewed, collected and studied by American scholars and artists from the turn of the century to the present. And finally, the physical characteristics which separate the transitional period blanket from the classic Rio Grande textile are described.

In Part Two, each blanket in the collection is depicted in photographs accompanied by a detailed analysis and description based on the information presented in the previous section.

The information which led to the identification of the textiles in the collection as Rio Grande blankets was obtained from three major sources. First, the published and unpublished literature were consulted. The most important publication to date, referred to by both weavers and historians alike as the standard reference work on Hispanic textiles of the Rio Grande Valley, is *Spanish Textile Tradition of New Mexico and Colorado*, edited by Nora Fisher.[3]

Second, more than three hundred Rio Grande textiles were examined. These are located in the Museum of International Folk Art in Santa Fe, New Mexico; The Taylor Museum in Colorado Springs, Colorado; the Albuquerque Museum in Albuquerque, New Mexico; and the Millicent Rogers Museum in Taos, New Mexico. They were compared with blankets in the collection.

Third, prominent Rio Grande textile scholars and contemporary weavers were interviewed. They offered expert assistance and individual criticism. Those interviewed include Helen R. Lucero, Curator of New Mexican Hispanic Crafts and Textiles, Museum of International Folk Art in Santa Fe; Maria Vergara Wilson, a weaver working in traditional Rio Grande textiles in La Madera, New Mexico; Juanita Jaramillo-Lavadie, a scholar and weaver in Taos, New Mexico; and David Ortega of Ortega's Weaving Shop in Chimayo, New Mexico.

It is hoped that this publication will help to place the transitional period Rio Grande blanket in its broader cultural and historical context, providing a vehicle for a growing understanding of this period in New Mexican history. The textiles themselves eloquently mirror the changes that took place in New Mexico in the last decades of the 1800s.

ACKNOWLEDGMENTS

THIS PROJECT would have been impossible without the help and encouragement of Mr. Will and the late Mrs. Liz Doty. They graciously allowed full access to their beautiful collection. They also granted permission for two exhibitions of their blankets, "The Rio Grande Blanket and the Coming of the Railroad" (Sept. 12 - Oct. 8, 1989) and "Rio Grande Blankets: Late Nineteeth-Century Textiles in Transition" (Aug. 28 - Dec. 20, 1992), both at the University Art Museum, University of New Mexico (UNM).

Of great personal help, support and encouragement were members of my graduate committee, Mary Grizzard, Chair, and Douglas George, who introduced me to the project, both of the Department of Art and Art History, and John L. Kessell of the Department of History, UNM.

Numerous individuals of various institutions were most generous with their time as well as with their advice and collections. Among these are Helen R. Lucero, Curator of New Mexican Hispanic Crafts and Textiles, Museum of International Folk Art, Santa Fe; Tom Lark, Curator of the Albuquerque Museum; Cathy Wright, Curator of The Taylor Museum of the Colorado Springs Fine Arts Center, Colorado; and Marian Rodee, Curator of Southwestern Ethnology at the Maxwell Museum of Anthropology, UNM.

Of invaluable help were the afternoons spent with Maria Vergara Wilson in La Madera, New Mexico and Juanita Jaramillo-Lavadie in Taos, New Mexico. Both offered new and interesting insights from the perspective of the weaver that I had not considered. Charles Carrillo was also very kind and helpful. He introduced me to David Ortega, of Chimayo, who filled my notebook with anecdotes and information on the Chimayo blanket.

My dear friends Susan Zamora and Therese Mulligan, of Albuquerque, and Rose Anne Enriquez, of El Paso, Texas, offered hours of much needed moral support. My aunt, Mary Anderson, of San Antonio, Texas, offered hours of editing and helpful suggestions for which I am most grateful. And most important, I wish to mention Eric Lane. He offered inspiration as he read every sentence for what must have seemed like hundreds of times. Thank you one and all.

This study was made possible, in part, by research grants provided by the Student Research Allocations Committee and the Vice President's Graduate Research Fund, both awarded through the Graduate Student Association, UNM, in 1988 and 1991, and the Center for Regional Studies through the Southwest Hispanic Research Institute, UNM, in 1991.

PART ONE

CHAPTER 1

Rio Grande Weaving: A Concise History

VARIETY IS THE KEY WORD in describing the geography of the Rio Grande Valley. In colonial times, the Rio Grande drainage system was divided into two parts by La Bajada Escarpment, a jagged lava outcropping about fifteen miles south of Santa Fe, New Mexico. Above this point was the Rio Arriba, extending north to the San Luis Valley in Southern Colorado. Below the escarpment was the Rio Abajo, the area south to Socorro, New Mexico.

Climatically the area is characterized by long cold winters and a relatively short growing season in the Rio Arriba, and a mild dry climate with a long growing season in the Rio Abajo. The terrain fluctuates from picturesque and rugged mountains capped by snow much of the year in the north, to arid desert with scarce vegetation in the south.

An occasionally interrupted narrow strip of arable land on both sides of the river and of its feeders and tributaries weaves an undulant band of lush *bosque*, suitable for farming of squash, beans, corn, cotton and chiles. Dry-land grazing is attempted on the sporadic rolling pasturage above the river valley where cattle, sheep, goats and horses have been raised from the early Spanish Colonial times to the present (Illustration 3, page 38).

Perhaps the feature most common to the entire area is the overall high degree of difficulty in mere survival encountered by all prehistoric and historic settlers.

By A.D. 1300 the river valley from north of Taos down to Socorro had been settled haphazardly by small groups of late prehistoric Pueblo Anasazi. Surviving at a bare subsistence level, they harvested corn, beans and squash and domesticated cotton from which they wove cotton *mantas*, a lightweight garment often ornamented with embroidery. They built clustered dwellings of masonry and puddled adobe, and subterranean pits, or kivas, for ritual practices.[4] And they were in possession of the land when Francisco Vásquez de Coronado arrived in 1540.

Ancestors of Hispanic Weaving in New Mexico

The Spaniards who landed in the New World came with a sophisticated textile tradition. Weavers and apprentices were formally organized in workshops (*obrajes*) under a guild system. The system was soon implanted in Mexico where *obrajes*, based on the Spanish model, were in place as early as 1550.[5]

New to America were Spanish technology and materials which soon influenced indigenous textile production in all parts of the new Spanish Empire. Technology included the cumbersome horizontal treadle loom, which had been introduced to Europe from the Near East around A.D. 1000 (Illustration 2, page 37). Its continuous warp allowed for a near endless length of yardage: pieces of cloth one hundred *varas* in length (one *vara* equals about 33 inches) were common.

New materials included wool from sheep, especially the common domestic variety called *churro*, introduced to the New World by the Spaniards along with cattle, horses and other animals. In the sixteenth century, sheep thrived, as did other livestock, due to the abundant availability of virgin pasturage. Accordingly, the woolen textile industry flourished, especially in Puebla and Texcoco, Mexico.

The Spanish Crown and its representatives continuously sought, among other things, new textile markets as well as new textile production centers throughout the 1500s. Initial exploration by Coronado and others of New Mexico established that the area was devoid of almost all natural resources but one: a ready supply of untapped labor. This factor contributed to the Spanish colonial expansion into New Mexico in the next century.

When the Spaniards arrived in the Rio Grande Valley in 1540, they discovered it to be inhabited by natives living in small clustered semi-agrarian settlements, or "pueblos."

The Pueblo men they encountered, according to Hernán Gallegos, chronicler for the Chamuscado-Rodríguez expedition (1581), "adorn themselves with pieces of colored [handspun] cotton cloth three-fourths of a *vara* in length and two-thirds in width, with which they cover their privy parts. Over this they wear, fastened at the shoulders, a blanket of the same material, decorated with many figures and colors, which reaches to their knees, . . . Some (in fact, most) wear cotton shirts, hand-painted and embroidered . . . Below the waist the women wear cotton skirts, colored and embroidered; and above, a blanket [*manta*] of the same material, figured and adorned like those used by the men . . . and [they] gird it with embroidered cotton sashes adorned with tassels"[6]

Woven on the indigenous upright loom, these practical and beautiful textiles, the *manta* especially, were destined to become one of two major tribute goods, or taxes, collected by the Spaniards from the Indians throughout the following century (the other being the staple food, maize).

Coronado, equipped for conquest rather than colonization, had little direct impact on the weaving practices of the pueblos. Over 5,000 sheep were brought into the area in this first *entrada*, but they were used as a food source on the hoof rather than as a ready wool supply. As Ward Alan Minge points out, the rugged country took its toll on the sheep population, but sufficient numbers survived to sustain the Spaniards, who carefully protected their dwindling herds. When Coronado departed in 1542, his chronicler, Pedro de Castañeda de Nájera, recorded that sheep were left behind at Pecos with Fray Luis de Úbeda. Subsequent conquistadors, however, did not mention sheep, which suggests that the animals may have soon perished.[7]

Colonial Hispanic Blanketry

The first real attempt at colonization, led by Don Juan de Oñate, was in 1598. With him came over 2,500 ewes and rams, yet the colonizers brought no looms and little handspun yarn, suggesting that the animals were once again intended solely as a food source.

Also, the Spaniards came laden with yard goods and ready-to-wear clothing, further proof that weaving was not yet a major consideration.[8] The list of tools and manpower suggests, however, that they did come with an ability to build looms as well as other necessities.[9]

The colonizers were well aware of the Indians' ability to produce cotton blankets. They collected them as tribute from the pueblos. Minge notes that Oñate was granted the power to assess taxes on the local Indians once they had vowed their allegiance to the Spanish Crown. The right to collect tribute (an *encomienda*) was granted to individual Spaniards as a way to support their military and colonizing efforts. Theoretically, to protect the pueblos from exploitation, the Franciscans were to supervise tribute collection.[10] As has often been repeated, tribute excess was common, a primary factor leading to the Pueblo Revolt of 1680.

Both the sheep and weaving industries progressed slowly through the first quarter of the century. Tribute of cotton *mantas* remained the colony's primary source of textiles, supplemented by an irregular flow of trade goods from Mexico.

The establishment of the missions, especially after 1625, had a profound influence on both sheep raising and weaving. As sheep numbers increased, wool became more plentiful. The Pueblo Indians were taught to weave with wool by the Franciscan friars, though they continued to use the indigenous upright loom. According to Joe Ben Wheat, a specialist in Spanish Colonial material culture, wool became the predominant fiber in pueblo weaving in the 1630s.[11]

Though ownership of business enterprises by the governor in New Mexico was officially prohibited, woolen cloth began to be produced in the illicit Santa Fe *obraje* owned by then current governor, Francisco Martínez Baeza (1634-37). He staffed the workshop with both Spanish and Indian labor.

His successor, Governor Luis de Rosas (1637-41), continued the practice. He also collected excessive tribute from the pueblos. Furthermore, Rosas was accused of seizing looms (the earliest known reference to the Spanish loom from the period) from private parties in order to corner the market on local textile production and to accumulate goods for trade with Mexico.[12]

Trade in textiles became an increasingly important issue as the century progressed. For example, Governor Bernardo López de Mendizábal (1659-1661) brought with him to New Mexico trade goods which he exchanged in kind with the Indians for *mantas* and other local products. He established a store in the Casa Real in Santa Fe from which he sold imported items to Spaniards, often on credit. Sometimes, Spaniards repaid their debt with their *encomienda* tribute by relinquishing their right to Mendizábal. Mendizábal, in turn, personally collected this tribute from the Indians. The amassed local textiles were then shipped to Mexico.[13]

Little is known about Spanish textile production in the seventeeth century. There is no direct evidence to prove that the Spanish loom was imported into seventeenth-century New Mexico. Yet, indirect evidence suggests its existence there.

As previously noted, the Spaniards possessed both the technology and tools with which to build the loom. And, judging from the reference to looms seized by Luis de Rosas, it is apparent that the Spanish loom was in use. Home production had increased sufficiently to yield some goods for export, thus the governor's attempt to quash the competition.

Also, as Dorothy Boyd Bowen indicates, an export invoice from 1538 lists *sayal* (woolen cloth) in lengths of 100 *varas*, a length impossible on the Indian upright loom. This further reinforces the theory that the Spanish loom was in use in the Hispanic New Mexican home at this time.[14]

By the time of the Pueblo Revolt in 1680, the Spanish textile industry in New Mexico had grown from indigenous local production to fledgling cottage industry. Exploited by the governor, the *encomendero* and the missionary under the tribute system, Indian weavers produced both cotton and woolen cloth on the upright loom.¹⁵ At the same time, Spanish weaving, in place by about 1630, increased as the century progressed.

Spanish textile production would experience a brief hiatus due to the revolt of 1680 when the Pueblo Indians drove the Spaniards out of New Mexico. It would resurface soon after the reconquest by Governor Don Diego de Vargas (1691-96).

The Eighteenth Century

On the heels of reconquest, colonization began anew, built upon the lessons learned from the experience of the revolt. The *encomienda* system, along with the requisite tribute, was abolished, thus freeing the Indians from this form of taxation. Indians who had fled the area and sought refuge with the Navajo and the Hopi to the west returned to the pueblos. Old traditions were resumed.

After the revolt, the Spanish government replaced the *encomienda* with the land grant. Minge identifies the land grant as the single most important factor in the establishment of a permanent colony in New Mexico. The land grant also encouraged the expansion of the sheep and wool production industries.¹⁶

For the first time, Spaniards were allowed to privately own land outside the villa of Santa Fe. This prompted settlers to return, and with them came livestock, especially important in the Rio Abajo with its plentiful water supply from the Rio Grande.¹⁷

It is here in the Rio Abajo that compelling direct evidence emerges, albeit late in the century, which reinforces the theory that the textile industry in colonial New Mexico experienced a period of growth in the 1700s. From analysis of the 1790 census records, which list sixty-four ranchers in the Rio Abajo, Bowen has identified the names and numbers of individuals involved in all aspects of textile production.

"... nearly one-third of the heads of family were involved in textile production, with fifty-five weavers, sixteen spinners, and thirty carders mentioned for Atrisco, Albuquerque, and Alameda alone. Another twenty-six weavers and five carders are listed in towns south of Albuquerque, along the Rio Grande from Pajarito to just below Belen, with the tiny village of Tome boasting seven weavers, two carders, and two tailors.... Unfortunately, not a single documented example of this once prolific Rio Abajo textile industry has come to light, although evidence from nineteeth-century *guías* (cargo lists) gives a vague suggestion of its characteristics."¹⁸

Further descriptions of the types of locally-produced textiles are derived from wills and inventories dated from 1750 to 1809. Some of these types are: *jerga* (floor covering), *sarapes* (wearing blankets), *frazadas* (bedding blankets), *mantas* (woolen and cotton shawls), *sabanilla* (woolen sheeting), *colchas* (embroidered bed covering) and stockings. Exact physical descriptions of these types of textiles have not yet come to light. But, by the mid-1700s, both Indian and Spanish weavers alike were weaving weft-faced plain weave striped *frazadas* and *sarapes* in natural yarns. Accent colors were provided by yarns dyed with indigo, a natural blue dye imported from Mexico.¹⁹

The *guías* from the annual trade caravans also indicate a brisk, if uneven, trade between Mexico and New Mexico throughout the century (as Minge notes, the larger share of trade went to Mexico).²⁰ Trade was hampered, however, by restrictive travel laws, the Indian threat and great distances.

In an attempt to encourage more trade between Mexico and the colony and to stimulate the local economy, Minge writes:

"... the governor of New Vizcaya recommended to the viceroy in Mexico City [Count Revilla Gigedo] the stimulation of sheep raising, the wool industry, and the cultivation of cotton.... [He suggested that] the governor in Santa Fe should set up a center for weaving common cloth, *manta*, [and] *bayeta* (flannel) ... Six craftsmen of each class should go to New Mexico from factories in Veracruz, Perote, and other places in order to start the weaving center. Also, they should take with them six *telares* (looms) for wool, six for *bayeta*, and six more for making *mantas*. . . . All these people and supplies should collect in Chihuahua by January [1789] in time to enter New Mexico with the annual military supply train." [21]

In response, Revilla "agreed with proposals instructing provinces to encourage more trade, to establish a weaving factory in Santa Fe, and to direct New Mexicans . . . to increase their herds and flocks."[22] Many of these proposals would be put into effect, to some degree, in the first two decades of the nineteenth century; and it is the result of these proposals that marks the coming of age of the textile industry in New Mexico.

The Nineteeth Century

As late as 1802, the recommendations made to Revilla had not yet been implemented. This is evidenced by New Mexico Governor Fernando Chacón's report to the king. In it, as described by Bowen, "Chacón noted the lack of an apprentice system, official examinations for master workmen, and *grémios* (guilds) like those found in New Spain, with their strict and explicit *Ordenanzas* (regulations)."[23] Chacón continued by listing the numerous textiles produced, supporting the existence of what Joe Ben Wheat calls a "moderate cottage industry" in eighteenth-century New Mexico.[24]

In reply, the government inaugurated an annual trade fair at El Paso. This significantly increased local access to southern trade. Furthermore, in an effort to improve local production, viceregal authorities sent master weavers Don Ignacio Ricardo Bazán and Don Juan Bazán to Santa Fe. From 1807 to 1809, the Bazán brothers taught weaving in Santa Fe, apparently with much success, for the student samples they sent to Mexico in 1809 were well received.[25]

Though documented proof remains undiscovered to link the brothers definitively to a new type of textile, the Saltillo-style, which emerged in Rio Grande weaving in the early decades of the century, most textile scholars postulate a connection between them. For example, Bowen surmises that "the Bazáns brought the technical knowledge needed to execute the complex designs found in contemporary Mexican *sarapes*, particularly in those beautiful, fine garments now known as 'Saltillo *sarapes*'."[26]

In his *Concise and Candid "Exposición" on the Province of New Mexico (1812)*, Don Pedro Bautista Pino, a merchant in Santa Fe and local representative to the Spanish *cortes* (parliament), credited Don Ignacio Bazán with "the introduction of fine looms for cotton [and wool?] . . . He has given instruction to many people in a remarkably short time. Although I call this fine weaving, I do so with reference to that which was formerly woven, for this fine cloth is hardly better than coarse goods in comparison with fine materials from China. . . . "[27]

According to Pino's report, textile trade along the Camino Real was expanding. He describes the great risks taken by traders to export surplus locally-made textiles, including blankets, quilts, sackcloth, cotton hose and table linens, to Mexico. It is apparent that weaving was experiencing an increase in both quantity and quality.

Design systems, or pattern plans, previously limited to the simple stripe (blanket 28) were expanded by the new design vocabulary borrowed from the Saltillo *sarape* of Mexico. The technology needed to produce the new style was perhaps, as previously noted, introduced to New Mexico by the Bazán brothers.

Though its origins remain obscure, the Mexican *sarape* is thought to have been indigenous to Mexico. A wearing blanket (poncho), it is characterized by its rectangular shape and center slit through which the wearer's head protrudes.

It was worn by "the Indians and mestizos of central Mexico [from about 1700 to 1850] . . . by all classes along the northern frontiers . . . [and] in a burst of nationalism [after Mexican independence in 1821] . . . by the *charros*—the upper-class Spaniards who devoted much time, money, and energy to horse culture."[28]

The Saltillo *sarape*, the most beautiful and intricately designed sub-type in the broader category of Mexican *sarape*, is distinguished by its central radiating serrate diamond or lozenge design set against a complex vertical background. The whole is framed by a continuous contrasting border (blanket 29).

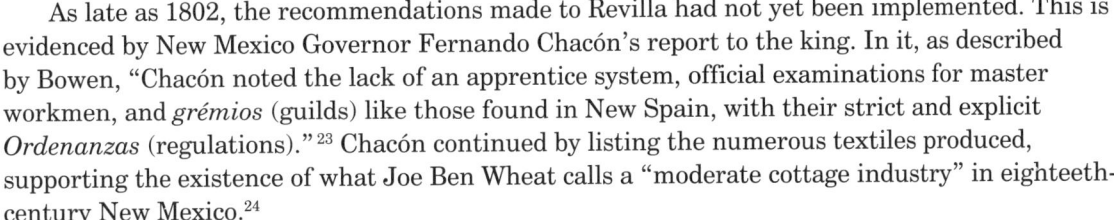

The design was apparently the result of a combination of several different traditions. Tlaxcalan families were ordered to the Saltillo region of Coahuila as a buffer between Spanish settlers and the renegade *Chichamecas*, native "wild Indians." These families brought with them a long weaving tradition from the Puebla area of Central Mexico. There, their own tradition had merged early with Spanish technology in the *obrajes*.

In Saltillo, new indigenous influences were incorporated by the Tlaxcalan weavers. The resultant Saltillo *sarape* was the finest example of weaving in the history of Mexican textiles.[29]

In New Mexico, the Saltillo *sarape* had a profound influence on local textile production. The basic design system was borrowed directly from the Saltillo *sarape*, but altered somewhat by the skill and understanding of the individual weaver and by the relative crudeness of the local version of the Spanish loom.

The Rio Grande Saltillo had a simpler background. It was made up of slightly larger, yet derivative, motifs. The central diamond radiated, though to a lesser degree than in the Saltillo *sarape*, and its edges were defined by larger serrations. Often the framing device was eliminated completely (blanket 30). Or, it was replaced by top and bottom bands of narrow stripes made up of all of the colors found in the blanket (blanket 31). Occasionally, vertical selvages (edges) were bordered with designs reminiscent of the Saltillo frame. But in the Rio Grande version, the frame was never completed on the top and bottom edges (blanket 32). This pattern, with much revision and alteration, continued to be woven into the twentieth century in New Mexico.

Saltillo-inspired design elements were also incorporated into the conventional Rio Grande band and stripe blanket, dating to the early 1700s. The design system of the band and stripe traditionally was composed of five or seven wide bands of narrow stripes. These were separated by narrower areas of solid color or contrasting narrow stripes (blanket 28). In the nineteenth-century variant, isolated design elements, such as chevrons, diamonds and hourglass, the leaf (*manita* or *palma*), and the meander, appeared in the wide bands (blanket 33). These were borrowed from the Saltillo *sarape*. This pattern persisted into the following century.

Textile production and trade accelerated in New Mexico after Mexico attained its independence from Spain in 1821. Previously closed borders between New Mexico and the United States opened. Trade was encouraged on both sides.

In New Mexico, this had a profound effect on the textile industry, especially in the Rio Arriba. According to Wheat, the opening of the Santa Fe Trail in 1821 encouraged trade with Missouri and points East. Coarse woolen blankets, cotton cloth and *jerga*, used to wrap bales of export goods, were sold.

The California market, via the Old Spanish Trail, opened in 1829. New Mexicans traded *frazadas* and *sarapes* for beaver skins and pelts from the Indians of California, and for mules and horses from Spanish *rancheros* (ranchers). Meanwhile, a brisk trade in textiles continued with the interior of Mexico until 1848.[30]

Anglo visitors to the area provided the first detailed descriptions of the Rio Grande blanket of this period and its use by individuals.

For example, Josiah Gregg, a Santa Fe trader from 1831 to 1840, described the New Mexican gentleman horseman (*caballero*), dressed in his low, wide brimmed hat (*sombrero*), embroidered jacket (*chaqueta*), trousers with a side slit decorated with silver buttons (*calzones*), and leather leggings (*botas*). He also had a fancy blanket, or "sarape saltillero.... This peculiarly useful as well as ornamental garment is carried dangling carelessly across the saddle, except in bad weather, when it is drawn over the shoulders ... or as is more frequently the case, the rider puts his head through a slit in the middle, and by letting it hang loosely from the neck, his whole person is protected."[31]

In 1846 Susan Magoffin, visiting New Mexico with her husband, described another interesting use for the *sarape*. She records that on the Santa Fe Trail she saw an Indian trader loaded down with "many things to sell." He wrapped his goods in a local *sarape*.[32]

Mexican domination of the area ended with American territorial annexation of New Mexico in 1848. American influences on New Mexican culture were apparent almost immediately.

By the early 1860s the importation of new materials and trade goods began to affect all aspects of Hispanic culture, including locally produced goods. Three new imports in particular altered the character of Rio Grande textiles forever.

First, in 1856, the invention of the first coal tar, or aniline, dye by the English chemist William Henry Perkin, sparked a revoluton in the dye industry. In New Mexico, aniline and, somewhat later, synthetic dyes began to be available in a rainbow of colors. More fugitive (fadeable) but less expensive and time-consuming than natural dyes, they allowed the weaver to broaden his once restricted palette.[33]

Second, with the arrival of comparatively inexpensive 3-ply synthetic-dyed Early Germantown yarns in about 1864, blankets woven completely of commercial yarns were not uncommon. Natural-dyed Saxony 3-ply commercial yarns were in use as early as 1821. Fisher and Wheat note, however, that the yarns were sparingly used. The Early Germantowns were available in a broad range of colors, but they lacked a pleasant sheen. This was not a problem with the second generation 4-ply Germantown yarns available after 1875.[34]

And third, the first Rambouillet-Merino sheep, a French strain, was introduced to northeastern New Mexico by the American military circa 1858. It yielded more meat than the *churro*, a feature particularly attractive to increasing numbers of Anglo sheep ranchers. Its short, kinky wool was preferred to that of the *churro* by commerical textile producers in the East. But, its wool was less suitable for hand processing. The Merino's greasy, and thus dirty fleece required large amounts of water for cleaning, a very significant drawback in an arid region.[35]

A less hearty breed, the Merino was ill-suited to rugged New Mexico, but its popularity increased with Anglo ranchers. By the 1880s, the Merino was common only in northeastern New Mexico. Ten years later, most *churro* stock had been highly contaminated.[36] The resultant wool lacked the soft sheen and even softer "hand," or feel, of pure *churro*, a factor often cited when textiles from this later period are compared to classic examples.

Blanket usage seems to have changed in this period as well, due to the influence of American dress. As noticed by Bowen, period photographs, beginning in about 1860, depicted a Spanish citizenry no longer dressed in the *sarape*. The *frazada*, on the other hand, continued in use as bed covering, *jerga* persisted as sacking.[37]

The opening of the Territorial Period (1848-1912) marked a general decline in trade relations with Mexico and California. The New Mexican textile industry, however, apparently suffered little from this loss in the early Territorial Period. Wheat, in his 1987 study of military reports in the United States National Archives, has convincingly demonstrated the emergence of an active military patronage.[38]

Under the American government's policy of Indian pacification, "bids were made on contracts. Agents for contractors scoured the [New Mexican] countryside for blankets."[39] Wheat reports that a minimum of 21,946 blankets, described generally as the band and stripe variety purchased from the Rio Arriba, were distributed to Native Americans from 1856-1874.[40]

When quality declined, purchases fell off, apparently after about 1875. Wheat cites United States documents, noting that the end of the market came when "a contract was let to furnish blankets with a thread count of at least four threads to the inch, but when the blankets supplied had only two ' . . . simply carded rolls of wool without being spun or twisted,' the blankets were rejected, and no more appear to have been requested."[41]

Consequently, by the time the railroad arrived in 1879, changes in production and trade of Rio Grande textiles were already apparent. This was due to the direct influence of the increasing American presence in the area.

Changes included an expanding and shifting trade which demanded increased production; the importation of new dyes that altered the once restrained color system of the Rio Grande weaver; and the availability of commercial yarns, which, along with the increasing contamination of the native *churro* by the Merino sheep, altered the texture of the traditional Rio Grande blanket.

The coming of the railroad not only accelerated change but it also introduced new variables. One important variable was the tourist market which would even further influence the course of Hispanic weaving in New Mexico. Its effect would be felt for decades.

CHAPTER 2

Impact of the Railroad and the Early Collectors

IN 1879, WHEN THE SANTA FE RAILROAD, pushing south from Trinidad, Colorado, reached Raton in the New Mexico Territory, it stirred up more than just dust. The railroad stirred up trade — it brought salesmen searching out new markets and hawking new wares. It stirred up tourists hungry for mementos of their trip "out West." And, it stirred up eastern academics seeking clues to Southwest traditions.

Some of the first people to step off the Santa Fe were Smithsonian ethnographers Jesse Walter Fewkes, James and Matilda Coxe Stevenson and George Brown Cooke. Their goal was to study and collect data on the Pueblo Indians of the New Mexico Territory. As they proceeded from pueblo to pueblo they acquired through purchase and trade what they believed were purely Indian artifacts.

Not all of the artifacts they collected were Native American. Labeled "Indian," a number actually represented the Hispanic craft traditions of New Mexico, including *santos*, or devotional images, and textiles.

As has been pointed out by Richard E. Ahlborn and Harry R. Rubenstein, artifacts collected by these ethnographers were confused with Indian artifacts, presumably because both had been collected in the pueblos. Photographs of the "Indian" displays in the Smithsonian's Arts and Industries Building, reproduced by Ahlborn and Rubenstein, attest to the confusion.[42]

The confusion was compounded by the profit motive of the traders. Buying from both Indian and Hispanic craftspeople alike, especially weavers, all goods were advertised as "Indian," regardless of the source. Indian crafts were in vogue back East. This confusion would persist into the early years of the twentieth century.

For example, Bertha P. Dutton noted that Herman Schweitzer, collector for the Fred Harvey Company from 1880 to 1930, kept few precise records. The origin and ethnicity of his early purchases for the Indian Arts Museum in the Alvarado Hotel, Albuquerque, one hotel in the company's string of many located along the Santa Fe Railroad, were not documented.

As can be seen in anonymous photographs of the Alvarado's interior (ca. 1906), examples of Native American and Hispanic, as well as Mexican art, are indiscriminately yet aesthetically arranged.[43] Hispanic *santos* are displayed next to Native American kachina dolls. More significantly, numerous Rio Grande and Indian textiles, weaving tools and materials are arranged haphazardly, as if cultural grouping were irrelevant. These photographs suggest that no real distinction among art-producing groups was being made (illustration 4, page 39).

The coming of the railroad had other, and perhaps more important effects on textiles. It brought cheap American imports from the eastern United States. These replaced the need for and the making of handmade blankets for domestic use by Hispanics and Native Americans alike.

It also brought the American tourist. American traders, quick to recognize a new market, began to advertise "Indian" blankets. Charlene Cerny and Christine Mather recognize this as a fusion of Indian and Hispanic blanketry.[44] These blankets, though similar in many respects, were produced by both Native American and Hispanic weavers on their respective traditional looms.

Textiles produced by Hispanics for the tourist trade came for the most part from the area just northwest of Santa Fe. These are now generally referred to as Chimayo textiles. Made of commercial yarns, they were woven on the Spanish loom by Hispanic weavers who borrowed heavily from traditional Rio Grande and Native American designs.

Through the first decade of the century, the Chimayo blanket remained indistinguishable from the Indian tourist blanket. As Yvonne Lange notes, the former was "attributed by prestigious museums to such non-existent groups as the 'Indians of Chemallo [Chimayó] Pueblo,' or to the 'Trampas Pueblo Indians'."[45]

Yet at least one collector and scholar was making the distinction. Lange reports that, as early as 1910, H. P. Mera (Curator of Archaeology at Santa Fe's Laboratory of Anthropology in the 1930s and '40s) began noticing the differences. In considering the origin and history of the Spanish-American horizontal loom and its associated nineteenth-century textiles, Dr. Mera pointed out "the vast differences between the twentieth-century Chimayó textiles and the nineteenth-century blankets and proposed the term 'Rio Grande blanket' for the latter."[46]

George Wharton James, in *Indian Blankets and Their Makers,* appears to be the first to publish a reference which distinguished between Native American and Hispanic blanketry. As Lange points out, James "recognized the 'Chimayó blanket' as a Spanish rather than an Indian product . . . [He] listed the differences between the nineteenth-century [Chimayó] and the contemporary commercial Chimayó textiles."[47]

A new awareness of and appreciation for the distinctiveness of Hispanic art began to surface in the second decade of this century. This was stimulated in part by the development of two related early twentieth-century architectural styles centered in Santa Fe: Spanish Pueblo and Mission Style Revival in public and domestic architecture.

The development of both trends, grouped together as Santa Fe Style, was economically motivated, aimed at installing Santa Fe as the premier tourist mecca in the Southwest. Aesthetic and utilitarian considerations were also important. Designers strove to create a style that was visually appealing as well as livable.

The first style was influenced by the New Mexico Pavilion built for the 1915 San Francisco Panama-Pacific Exposition. Its design was based on pueblo architecture. The first major influential expression of Spanish Pueblo Revival architecture in New Mexico was Santa Fe's Museum of Fine Arts (1917-18).[48]

More important to Hispanic blanketry, however, is the second trend, the Mission Style. It was influenced by Mexican colonial architecture. This included the Mexican hacienda, a largely self-sufficient rural residence with an open central patio and linear room arrangement. It was built throughout the colonial period by wealthy landowners in Mexico.

As an already existing tradition, the colonial New Mexican hacienda was believed to have been built in New Mexico by landed Hispanics during the colonial and postcolonial periods. The form was chosen by the *intelligencia* of Santa Fe as an appropriate prototype for new home construction. It was believed to have been visually and thematically, if not historically, harmonious with the Pueblo Revival style in public architecture. John Gaw Meem, a young civil engineer in Santa Fe by 1920, soon became the court architect to the Santa Fe art colony, designing numerous homes in Santa Fe in the new style.

The new style demanded not only appropriate exterior detailing, but suitable interior decoration as well. This in turn fostered a new interest in traditional Hispanic arts and crafts, including Hispanic weaving.

Collecting Became the Rage

While most references to early collecting of traditional Hispanic arts dealt specifically with *santos*, textiles were also important decorative items used as furniture throws, floor coverings and wall hangings.[49] At the early stages of collecting, however, distinctions between Hispanic and Native American blankets were less apparent than for other crafts. Photographs of period interiors show a casual mixing of the two textile types (illustration 5, page 39).

By the mid-twenties, collecting of traditional Hispanic art was well established in Taos and Santa Fe. Major collectors, notably Mary Austin and Frank Applegate, held long discussions with one another on their collections, eventually stimulating the revival of all traditional crafts.

As Marta Weigle notes from Austin's own writings, Austin and Applegate recognized the raw and untapped talent of local workers hired by them to repair broken or dilapidated items in their collections. They began to discuss the possibility of reviving traditional crafts. They organized a loosely formed support group, the Society for the Revival of the Spanish-Colonial Arts. It was incorporated in Santa Fe on October 15, 1929, as the Spanish Colonial Arts Society.[50]

The Society's greatest contributions were the preservation of traditional artifacts and the encouragement of new production in the traditional crafts. This included the making of *santos*, tin work, furniture carving, blanketry and other textile arts. The Society sponsored the annual Santa Fe Fiesta arts fair, begun in 1926, and named the Spanish Market in 1928. By that year, $300 was offered in prizes for textile arts and other traditional crafts, thereby encouraging wider Hispanic participation.[51]

Geared toward the discovery and encouragement of the individual craftsperson, the informal revival of Hispanic crafts in the late twenties was transformed in the next decade into a comparatively structured revival. It was no longer under the sole patronage of the *intelligencia*.

New retail outlets, the earliest sponsored by the Society, opened. Catering to the tourist, they specialized in local crafts. At the same time, Depression-era attempts to stimulate the local economy looked toward community projects in the form of vocational training in the traditional crafts. And, finally, federally funded cultural studies further increased non-Hispanic appreciation of traditional Hispanic arts.

In 1930, the Society opened a year-round store, the Colonial Arts Shop, in Santa Fe. Its purpose was not only to show and to sell traditional textile arts, but also to encourage personal experimentation. Unfortunately, the shop closed in 1933.

It was succeeded in the following year by the Native Market. The Market was highly successful through 1939, offering a broader spectrum of New Mexican crafts. This included furniture, woodcarvings and tinwork. With craftspeople actually working in the shop, the Market became a natural tourist attraction[52] (Illustration 6, page 39).

The Market's success inspired the opening of other outlets. Among these were Santa Fe's McCrossen Handwoven Textiles, Burro Weavers and Santa Fe Handwoven Fabrics, though, as Helen R. Lucero states, "most of the weaving produced by these concerns consisted of suiting and tie fabrics rather than blankets woven in the Hispanic tradition." The companies did, however, hire New Mexican weavers, most of whom came from the northern section of the state[53] (illustration 7, page 38).

Many of these Northern New Mexico weavers were trained at the state-run vocational schools. Cerny and Mather note that El Rito Normal School had a well-developed weaving program by 1930.[54] (illustration 8, page 39)

The school patterned its textile designs after traditional rather than twentieth-century Chimayo weavings. Its instructors adapted the shape and size of the textiles to modern usage, which included drapery, pillow shams, ties and other articles of clothing.[55] Baizerman notes that under the guidance of Brice Sewell, State Supervisor of Trade and Industrial Education (1933-43), El Rito became the model for vocational schools throughout rural New Mexico.[56]

Revival of Hispanic Weaving

By the middle of the 1930s, it would seem that weaving, in the traditional sense, had experienced a rebirth in the Hispanic community. This is well illustrated by the proliferation of new weaving outlets, shops and schools. But period documentation, notably the inconclusive government-sponsored Tewa Basin Study of 1935, contradicts the notion of a revival.[57] The study points toward only minimal participation by the rural nothern New Mexico Hispanic communities. It also indicates that much of what was produced was intended for home use. Most commerical participation, on the other hand, was centered around Chimayo, just northeast of Santa Fe.

The uneven quality of the published study, and the failure to adhere to a standardized form for the communities canvased, might imply inconsistent or even inaccurate record-keeping. Lucero feels that this discrepancy might have been due to the fact that northern weavers who worked in the shops of Santa Fe were not counted, reflecting a limited view on the part of the interviewers conducting the study.[58]

The government also sponsored the Historic American Building Survey (HABS) of the mid-1930s. Established under the Historic Sites Act of 1935, its goals were to measure systematically all regional landmarks across the United States and to document them historically. In New Mexico the study included both prehistoric and historic Indian sites as well as Hispanic sites. It drew upon the expertise of nationally renowned archaeologists and architectural historians. Immediate impact of the survey on the study of New Mexicana was forestalled by the events of World War II. But its long-range effects were phenomenal. The survey encouraged the appreciation of New Mexican regionalism; it further distinguished between Hispanic and Indian art; it suggested relationships in the art of these two cultural groups; and it stimulated scholarly interest in New Mexicana in general, indirectly affecting the quality and direction of all subsequent scholarship.

More directly related, however, was a third government-backed study, the 1937-38 *Portfolio of Spanish Colonial Design in New Mexico*. The publication grew out of the Works Projects Administration's Federal Art Project (FAP) in New Mexico and was, as Claudia Larcombe describes it, "a forerunner of and contributor to the national Index of American Design, both of which were established to record information on and the appearance of objects — among them furniture, pottery, metalwork, and textiles produced by Americans of European descent." [59]

The publication had a limited edition of 200, most of which were removed from circulation due to legal complications, thus the impact on the general public was minimal.[60] Yet it does represent the first sanctioned, if somewhat weak attempt to identify traditional arts and crafts in New Mexico as Hispanic, and it remains basic to any historical study on New Mexicana.

To summarize, the first four decades of the twentieth century were critical in fixing the direction of and opportunity for future Spanish Colonial scholarship. During this period an intellectual environment was established out of which the scholarship of the next fifty years would emerge.

As has been demonstrated, the nurturing evolved rapidly in these first four decades. Stimulated by architectural revivals which demanded appropriate interior design, near ignorance about Hispanic art of the first decade gave way to frenzied collecting and limited connoisseurship in the second decade of this century. In the next decade, these same collectors offered individual patronage and encouraged a revival of tradition, in turn paving the way for the government-sanctioned regionalism and revivalism of the thirties.

The private collections of traditional Hispanic arts amassed throughout the period would eventually become the core collections of major museums, and would be destined for in-depth research in the subsequent decades.

CHAPTER 3

Modern Criticism and Scholarship

SCHOLARLY INTEREST in New Mexican Spanish Colonial and Postcolonial art is of recent vintage, its seeds sown in the fertile intellectual environment of the first four decades of the twentieth century. Late nineteenth- and early twentieth-century confusion between Hispanic and Native American artifacts, brought on by indiscriminate collecting by American ethnographers, gave way to connoisseurship in the teens and twenties. Collectors, at first in search of Hispanic craftspeople to repair damaged articles, recognized the latent talent of these artisans, and encouraged a revival of traditional crafts through the twenties.

In the following decade, revival was further nurtured by Depression-era economic programs developed to stimulate local economies through support of vocational education in the traditional arts. Important, too, were other government-supported programs, such as the Historic American Building Survey and the Federal Art Project, which brought to New Mexico outside specialists, including artists, archaeologists and historians, many of whom became enamored of New Mexicana and either remained or returned periodically to research and write about it.

Early Research: 1940s - 1960s

In New Mexico research into all things New Mexican, interrupted briefly by the events of World War II, resumed in the late 1940s. Emphasis through the 1960s was placed on archival research, iconography and scientific analysis. The trend was best illustrated by Boyd's early work on the art of the *santero* (maker of *santos*), *Saints and Saint Makers of New Mexico*. In the introduction, she listed four goals for her investigation, a model used for research into New Mexicana throughout the next two decades. Boyd's goals were to: (1) reconstruct the historical background; (2) identify major subjects; (3) identify major centers of production; and (4) classify the *santos* typologically. [61] These same goals defined the evolution of her scholarship until her death in 1974.

Mera, who was certainly aware of Boyd's research because the two had worked closely together at the School of American Research at the Museum of New Mexico in Santa Fe, applied Boyd's paradigm to his own research on Hispanic textiles. He coined the term "Rio Grande blanket."

In his monograph, "Spanish-American Blanketry: Its Relationship to Aboriginal Weaving in the Southwest," Mera proved that these textiles were neither produced by Pueblo or Navajo weavers, nor were they derivative of Native American textiles. It is from this first major study that all subsequent research evolved.[62]

As suggested by Mera's research, the Rio Grande revival, begun in the twenties, continued to be a viable form in the forties. Numerous articles in *New Mexico Magazine*, by Ina Sizer Cassidy and others, supported Mera's observations.[63] In these articles specific artists, weaving centers, exhibitions and marketing were described. Also important in this decade was the article by William H. Dusenberg, "Woolen Manufacture in New Spain," an exploration of colonial wool technology in Mexico, important to the understanding of the economic side of sheep herding in New Mexico.[64]

Peripheral publications from the next two decades provided comparative analyses of the various Rio Grande types with their sources and influence. The Mexican Saltillo was studied in depth by Catherine Drew Jenkins in *An Analysis of the Saltillo Style in Mexican "Sarapes,"* a publication that continues as a model for textile research.[65] The research into Navajo textiles begun by Mera before 1950 expanded under Kate Peck Kent in *Navajo Weaving*.

Publications on Southwestern textiles proliferated through the end of the sixties. This trend culminated in a major travelling exhibition of more than one hundred Southwestern textiles from The Taylor Museum collection in Colorado Springs, Colorado.

A catalogue by Martha Tilley, titled *Three Textile Traditions: Pueblo, Navajo, and Rio Grande*, accompanied the exhibition.[66] Though this publication offered no new insight into Southwestern textiles, the text did summarize research to 1967, unfortunately, without citations.

Revivalism and Scholarship: 1970s

The decade of the seventies was one of expanding interest in colonial New Mexicana. This in turn fostered a resurgence of the revival of traditional-style Hispanic arts, especially under the influence and encouragement of Boyd through the expanding Spanish Colonial Arts Society in Santa Fe, New Mexico.[67]

The landmark publication of the period was Boyd's *Popular Arts of Spanish New Mexico*,[68] the culmination of the author's four decades of work in New Mexico. Her book probably rekindled revivals across the broad spectrum of traditional Hispanic arts. If it was not the actual catalyst, it certainly gave strong impetus to the movement.

In *Popular Arts*, Boyd dealt with all issues of Spanish colonial art, including *santos*, architecture and textiles. In her extensive chapter on textiles, she attempted to establish a chronological order for design systems as identified by Mera. Her model failed, to some degree, because of incorrect documentation of certain historical facts, which are now known. Though Boyd broke new ground, her model was ignored in much of the literature immediately following publication.

Hispanic Crafts of the Southwest, edited by William Wroth, formally Director of The Taylor Museum, reflected Hispanic revivals in the 1970s. His book, a collection of essays dealing with various aspects of twentieth-century art production by Hispanic artisans in New Mexico, accompanied a traveling exhibition of the same name. This exhibition brought contemporary New Mexican arts and crafts to cities such as Williamsburg, Virginia, and Kansas City, Missouri.[69] Included in this publication was an essay by Juanita Jaramillo-Lavadie, "Rio Grande Weaving: A Continuing Tradition." Jaramillo-Lavadie explored the work of modern weavers in New Mexico working in the colonial weaving tradition.[70]

A pivotal work in the understanding of the Hispanic community and its psychological and philosophical outlook was that of Thomas J. Steele, S.J. *"Santos" and Saints: Essays and Handbook*.[71] In it the author placed the art of the nineteenth- and twentieth-century *santero* within its social context. The book's implication for the subsequent study of all Hispanic art in New Mexico was readily apparent. Placed in context, the art was no longer viewed as mere object separate from the environment within which it was made.

Numerous cultural and anthropological studies from the 1970s aid in the understanding of that context. Marta Weigle's *Hispanic Villages of Northern New Mexico*, a reprint of Vol. II of the 1935 "Tewa Basin Study" of thirty-four Hispanic villages of Northern New Mexico, provided names of weavers and other artisans practicing traditional arts in the area at the time of the survey.[72]

Several exhibition publications from the 1970s on the Navajo blanket were important for comparative analyses. Works by J.J. Brody, Mary Hunt Kahlenberg and Anthony Berlant, and Marian Rodee, to name only a few, reflected the ever-increasing interest in Southwestern textiles.[73]

Periodical literature, also indicative of this expanding awareness, contributed much to the pool of information. Articles by Jean M. Burroughs, R.A. Donkin, J. Ehly and others addressed issues related to textile production such as colonial pastoralism, dye analysis and the contemporary textile market, respectively.[74]

Two unpublished manuscripts also proved invaluable: Marianne L. Stoller's "A Study of Nineteeth-Century Hispanic Arts and Crafts in the American Southwest: Appearances and Processes," and Wheat's "Spanish Weaving Terms Used in the Documents."[75]

The 1970s may be viewed as a great watershed in the study of colonial and postcolonial Hispanic arts and crafts in general, and weaving in particular. The decade ended with the publication of a book which gathered together under one cover all of the previous independent research on Hispanic textiles, placing them in cultural and historical context. The book, *Spanish Textile Tradition of New Mexico and Colorado*, edited by Nora Fisher, Curator of Textiles at the Museum of International Folk Art, was a collaborative effort by some of the most important scholars on Hispanic weaving in the Southwest.

Initially proposed as a project by Boyd, *Spanish Textile Tradition* may be viewed as an encyclopedic survey of Hispanic textile research up to 1979. Drawing heavily on Mera and Boyd, the various authors standardized basic nomenclature and design analyses, standards which continue to the present.

Though the blanket categorization standardized in *Spanish Textile Tradition* offered a handy tool for identification of colonial and postcolonial Hispanic textile types, certain inconsistencies and omissions suggested further scrutiny. For example, the criteria chosen to establish the various categories were dissimilar, based on design analysis for some, on materials and function for others.

Conspicuously absent in the text was a category for post-1880 blankets. With the exception of the Vallero and the Chimayo, these blankets were well within the traditional design vocabulary but were woven from non-traditional materials made available, for the most part, after the arrival of the railroad. They were characterized as inferior to classic blankets made from 1820 to about 1880.[76]

Specialized and Interdisciplinary Study: 1980s

In the 1980s, specialized and interdisciplinary studies broadened the research base established by *Spanish Textile Tradition*. Kent provided the criteria for distinguishing between the various types of Southwestern blanketry in "Spanish, Navajo, or Pueblo? A Guide to the

Identification of Nineteeth-Century Southwestern Textiles." Her criteria were based upon those established by the School of American Research in 1980-81.[77]

In "Early Trade and Commerce in Southwestern Textiles Before the Curio Shop," Wheat discussed heretofore unaddressed issues of nineteenth-century marketing and military patronage of the Rio Grande band and stripe blanket.[78]

Practical matters of colonial weaving technology and technique were researched in two unpublished manuscripts. In the first, a manuscript funded by a grant from the National Endownment for the Arts, Jaramillo-Lavadie chronicled the actual weaving of modern Rio Grande-style textiles in traditional methods and materials. In the second manuscript, Maria Vergara Wilson offered a practical handbook on traditional technology.[79]

Of increasing interest was the issue of the influence of tourism and Anglo patronage on textile production at the turn of the century. Two unpublished related texts, the first by Helen R. Lucero, the second by Suzanne Baizerman, offered research on two traditional weaving centers in New Mexico affected by outside influence. For both researchers, familial lineage and heritage, along with Anglo patronage and influence, defined Hispanic textile production in twentieth-century New Mexico.[80]

Lucero, in "Hispanic Weavers of North Central New Mexico: Social/Historical and Educational Dimensions of a Continuing Artistic Tradition," provided an interdisciplinary study of twenty modern weavers in the Rio Arriba and Taos areas of New Mexico. Especially important were Lucero's lineage charts for these twenty weavers. For some of these weavers, the family weaving tradition may be traced back for five generations. The author also included important information on the government-sponsored craft education programs of the 1930s.

In "Textiles, Traditions, and Tourist Art: Hispanic Weaving in Northern New Mexico," Baizerman defined the relationship between traditional ethnic art and its modern counterpart, "tourist art," in her case study of the weavers of Chimayo. Her primary sources included trade invoices and personal correspondence of Jake Gold and J.S. Candelario, traders in Santa Fe at the turn of the century who dealt in local native crafts, including Rio Grande blankets.

What does the future hold for the study of the Rio Grande blanket? At present, research is in progress into various aspects of the subject. Wheat continues to investigate issues of nineteeth-century patronage and production. Jaramillo-Lavadie and Vergara Wilson proceed with their experimentation with traditional technology and technique, as does Charles Carrillo, a *santero* and Southwestern anthropologist who is concerned with natural dyes and pigments.

In the planning stages, the joint publication by Lucero and Baizerman of their respective dissertations will also serve to encourage more research on Hispanic weaving.

The increasing interest in Rio Grande blankets was certainly one reason for the timely opening of "Los Colores," a public museum founded in 1989. "Los Colores" presents changing exhibitions of traditional and contemporary Mexican and New Mexican textiles in the atmosphere of the historic Alehandro Gonzales house in Corrales, New Mexico.

Perhaps the most stimulating recent force is the permanent installation of colonial arts and crafts in the Hispanic Heritage Wing, Museum of International Folk Arts, Santa Fe.[81] This exhibition is, to date, considered to be the most exact in terms of historic and contextual accuracy, and will surely serve to foster new issues for investigation.

Yet to be identified are individual weavers and specific weaving villages and centers. The process is being facilitated by the use of computer analysis and cataloguing of museum collections of Rio Grande blankets. It is hoped that computer analysis might identify sub-categories within the broad Rio Grande design classification system. Also unanswered are certain patronage and marketing questions. The field remains open to the creative researcher.

CHAPTER 4

The Transitional Period Rio Grande Blanket

IN THE LATTER PART of the nineteenth century, certain observable physical changes occurred in the Rio Grande blanket, changes which suggest periodic evolution of the craft.[82] It is the goal of this chapter to review these changes and to illustrate them by citing appropriate examples presented in "Part II: The Catalogue" of this book.

The change from classic to transitional blanketry was marked by the increasing availability of new materials which began to trickle into New Mexico as early as 1821 with the opening of the Santa Fe Trail. The trickle became a stream by mid-century and a flood by 1880 with the arrival of the railroad in the territory.

Modifications in the classic Rio Grande blanket began to be noticeable by about 1860, after the introduction of the Rambouillet-Merino sheep.[83] As previously noted, the Merino, preferred in the East as the best source of wool for machine carding and spinning, produced short, kinky, greasy fibers less suitable to handspinning than that of the traditional *churro*. By contrast, the *churro*, introduced to New Mexico by the Spaniards in the seventeeth century, produced long, silky fiber, perfect for handspinning. The fiber was also less oily, and thus cleaner, an important feature in arid New Mexico where water to wash wool was considered a luxury.[84] Merino soon began to be bred with *churro*, the resultant wool increasingly more Merino than *churro* in character as the century neared its end.[85] Thus, the blankets in this collection with a softer, silkier sheen are predominatly *churro* (blankets 1, 4 and 5), those with a duller matte finish are predominantly Merino (blankets 13, 18, 19 and 21). Yarns of both types are identifiable in blanket 3.

An expanding color palette also became apparent by 1860, and common after 1880. The classic Rio Grande blanket was woven of predominantly natural wool fibers. The *churro* ranged in color from a pale off-white to deep grays and browns. The palette was often enlivened by expensive dyes imported from Mexico, notably indigo and *cochineal* (red), which were sparingly used.[86] In this collection, only one blanket is datable to the classic period. Blanket 1 is a classic striped example woven of natural handspun *churro* (compare with blanket 28). The predominant color is natural dark brown, with natural white and indigo blue accent stripes, a common pattern datable to pre-1860. It is a fragment, mended perhaps by a trader or collector, and was once a five- or seven-band blanket, its worn center area removed, and the undamaged ends rewoven.

In blanket 21, the selection by the weaver of natural white, indigo and red yarns refers back to this simple classic color combination, a nostalgic recollection typical of the transitional period.[87]

The classic palette was also broadened somewhat by the use of natural dyes locally obtained, though these seem to have been used to a lesser extent than previously supposed. The collection and extraction of local dyes from plants and mineral sources were a labor intensive operation, thus the scarcity of natural dyed yarns in extant examples.[88] No natural dyes, with the exception of imported indigo, have been identified in this collection.

Commercial synthetic dyes began to arrive in New Mexico in the late 1860s.[89] Easy and quick, especially when compared to using natural dyes, synthetic colors rapidly became the dyes of choice among Hispanic weavers, opening up their once restrained palette. Riotous combinations of deep purple, acid green, hot red and violet vibrate across the surface of the traditionally inspired striped pattern.[90] Numerous examples of these are to be found in the collection, though their colors are often not as brilliant as when originally woven, owing to the fugitive nature of some synthetic dyes, especially intense greens, reds and violets, and, perhaps, to the inexperience of the dyer with the new techniques.

In the collection, transitional striped blankets woven of natural handspun yarns synthetically dyed that have suffered significant synthetic color loss include blankets 2, 4, 7, 8, 10 and 12; moderate fading is evident in blankets 3, 6, 11, 13, 16, 18 and 19; minimal fading is apparent in blankets 9, 14 and 15.

Saltillo-style blankets (Baizerman called these classic tapestries),[91] woven with an intricate design system borrowed from Mexico early in the nineteenth century (blanket 28), continued to be woven in the transitional period, and became seemingly more complex as the use of vibrant synthetic color increased (blankets 30-33). In the collection, transitional tapestries are represented by two examples. Blanket 20 is a band and stripe blanket with Saltillo design elements, as defined by Bowen in *Spanish Textile Tradition*. Each of the seven regular bands of red, green and natural brown stripes is energized by a center stripe composed of Saltillo inspired motifs: the outer two center stripes contain the Saltillo leaf, the inner three boast *palmitas*.[92] Blanket 22 might be described as a "blanket-within-a-blanket": the center Saltillo-style radiating serrate diamond is enclosed by an especially wide frame, a transitional adaptation of the thin framing device characteristic of classic tapestries.[93] In both, moderate fading is evident. However, if the original brilliant and disturbing color combinations of red, yellow-green, orange and violet in blanket 20 and red-orange, acid green and yellow in blanket 22 are imagined, intense color vibration may be visualized. It is this vibration which further complicates the intricate patterning of the Saltillo-inspired design.

Commercial Yarns

New materials, which began to arrive after the opening of the Santa Fe Trail, altered Hispanic blanketry as well. The classic Rio Grande was woven of handcarded, handspun local wool. Natural-dyed commercial yarns began to arrive early in the century.[94] Saxony, a fine three-ply yarn, was used for color accents by the Hispanic weaver in the 1820s and continued to be imported into New Mexico until about 1865. None of the blankets in the collection contain Saxony yarns.

Synthetic-dyed commercial yarns began to arrive in the 1860s, and were common after 1880. Their use was often discouraged by the trader after the turn of the century due to a tourist preference for handspun yarns.

The most common type was Germantown yarn, especially important to the weavers of Chimayo. Early Germantown yarn, a three-ply synthetic-dyed yarn, was imported from mills in the area around Germantown, Pennsylvania between 1864 and 1875. In a broad range of colors, Early Germantown yarns tended to be harsh in feel and somewhat lusterless. Blanket 24, an excellent example of Early Germantown, is a Chimayo furniture scarf, a new form designed for the tourist market.

A four-ply yarn, in an even wider range of colors, was introduced around 1875 and continues in use to the present. Fisher and Wheat note that this type replaced the earlier three-ply variety.[95] No examples of 4-ply Germantown yarns have been identified in the collection.

Chimayo blankets 25 and 26 are problematic in terms of yarn identification. David Ortega of Chimayo, identified both as having been woven of 3-ply Clasgens yarns, about which little has been written.[96] Dating of these blankets on design analysis and color selection alone, however, suggests that blanket 25 is an Early Chimayo. Its muted palette and flattened, drawn out pattern (due to its high thread count) indicate a production date of 1890-1900.

Blanket 26, because of its Pan-Southwestern motifs and brilliant palette, is a Modern Chimayo, ca. 1910-30. The bold Navajo-inspired central pattern dominates the composition, yet the Vallero-style framing device points to a Hispanic weaver, as does the weaving technique: it was woven on a Spanish horizontal loom.

Substitution of commmerical cotton twine for traditional handspun wool warp also marked the period change. Strong, inexpensive and readily available via the railroad, the use of commercial cotton warp allowed the weaver even more time to concentrate on the actual weaving process itself.[97] Cotton warp was used in transitional blankets 5, 7-9, 11-19 and 21 and Early Chimayo blanket 24. Moreover, cotton twine, perhaps because of its strength, was used in two examples to repair broken wool warps (blankets 3 and 4). Though the use of cotton warp was discouraged by the traders after 1900, its use was not uncommon after that date, as shown by its presence in Modern Chimayo blanket 25, and in the two revival blankets 23 and 27, produced around 1930.

Subtle pattern changes occurred in the transitional period as well. Classic Rio Grande blankets tended to be of three basic types. These were: (1) the simple band and stripe, referred to by Baizerman as classic striped (blanket 28); (2) the complex Saltillo-style (blankets 30-32); and (3) a combined variant: bands and stripes with isolated Saltillo elements (blanket 33).[98] Baizerman combined the second and third types under the general label "classic tapestry," a reference to technique.[99]

In the transitional period all three types of classic patterns were woven, though altered somewhat by the availability of new dyes and yarns. Simple striped examples include blankets 2-19. Blankets 20-23 are Saltillo-style. Classic patterns continued into the revival period as well, as evidenced by the Saltillo influenced pattern of blanket 23, and the classic-like striped design of blanket 27.

Though these design systems persisted into the transitional period, by the late 1800s the weaver felt freer to toy with tradition. Classic striped blankets were normally composed of five or seven bands of narrow variegated stripes, a pattern which continued into the transitional period (blankets 3-6, 9, 14 and 16). Yet in the later period, bands may increase to nine or more (blanket 13). Stripes may also vary more, from highly regular (blankets 2, 3, 6, 8, 11, 13, and 18) to erratic widths (blanket 14). They may dominate the blanket. Variations such as the Vallero,[100] with its eight-point star (not represented in this collection) or the Chimayo, an eclectic combination of traditional Hispanic and Indian motifs (blankets 24-26), began to appear.[101]

Personal expression in terms of design selection seems to have taken precedence over strict adherance to traditional designs. Two reasons for this appear plausible. The weaver may have been looking at other textiles imported from the East, as was probably the case with the Vallero, perhaps influenced by American quilts. Or, because of a growing trend in trade, a family's heirloom blankets became marketable, removing the best examples of traditional designs from the home. Weaving was learned through copying and emulation. If the weaver no longer had traditional examples from which to learn the craft, the weaver could improvise.[102]

Dimensions of the Rio Grande blanket varied only slightly from classic to traditional examples. Because of the narrow width of the Spanish horizontal loom, classic textiles were never wider than 56 to 71 cm. (26 to 28 in.).[103] Two methods were employed to enlarge the textile to a more functional width. The blanket may be woven as two separate halves, requiring planning and forethought so that the designs matched when the halves were stitched together with a handsewn center dovetailed seam.

The second and technically more complex method, called double width, involved the double warping of the loom, one layer over the other. Irene Emery, in *Primary Structures of Fabrics*, describes this method: "If the weft is continuous but always interweaves twice (over and back) with the warps of one layer before shifting to the other layer, the two layers of the fabric will be joined by the common weft only along one edge and, when removed from the loom, will spread to form a single simple weave fabric double the width of the loom. Thus it is only the construction method that is double, not the finished fabric."[104]

With the coming of the railroad, new technology, notably the wider reed, increased the capability of the Spanish loom. Transitional blankets without a center seam or double-weave ridge could be as wide as 138 cm. (55 in.) or more.[105] In this collection no transitional example has been identified, but blanket 24 (133 cm.; 52.5 in. wide), a revival tapestry, was woven either on a loom with a wider reed, or more probably, on a wider modern loom, available after 1890.[106] The Early Chimayo blanket 25 (121 cm.; 47.5 in. wide), is another example of this new technology.

Length was more dependent on function than on technology. The horizontal loom allowed for storage of an almost endless length of warp, thus the length of the finished blanket was determined by the individual weaver, and could vary between 171 cm. (67 in.) and 261 cm. (103 in.). Often the width to length ratio, however, was 1:1.5.[107] With the exception of Chimayo tourist variants, the length of the late nineteenth-century blanket remained well within these limits, though the width to length ratio varied sightly from the classic norm.

With the opening of the tourist market, new types of Rio Grande blankets came into being. Especially important was the weaving of Chimayo, geared to the needs of the tourist (such as blanket 24), began to be produced, and continue to be woven to the present.[108]

Although transitional period Rio Grande blanketry has previously been characterized in the literature as being poorly woven of second-rate materials, the blanketry itself bespeaks change and ingenuity on the part of the weaver. It is only recently that scholars have begun to reconsider their assessment of transitional textiles.

The nineteenth-century Hispanic weaver, much like the contemporary Navajo weaver, experimented with new labor-saving materials and technology increasingly available as the century progressed. The resultant changes which occurred in the textiles, however, were well within the traditional classic vocabulary. The textiles of this period represent a commingling of two cultures through the merging of traditional Hispanic craft with Yankee ingenuity and materials marked especially by the arrival of the railroad to New Mexico in 1879-80.

CHAPTER 5

Historic Photographs

2. *Spaniards wove on a horizontal treadle loom of European ancestry. The New Mexican version was made of rough, hand-adzed lumber. Preparing this cumbersome loom for weaving required two people.*
Photo by Ben Wittick. Courtesy School of American Research Collections in the Museum of New Mexico.

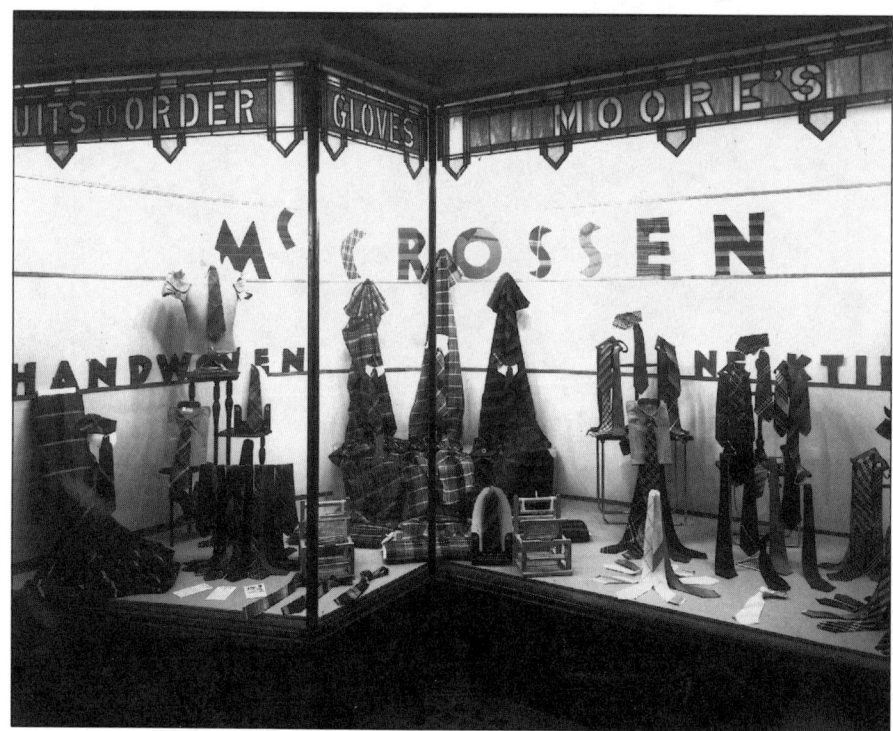

7. *Store window display of Moore's Men Shop, San Francisco Street, Santa Fe, New Mexico, ca. 1935. This textile outlet in Santa Fe, along with others such as McCrossen Hand-woven Textiles and Burro Weavers, carried suiting and tie fabrics made by Hispanic weavers.*
Photo by T. Harmon Parkhurst.
Courtesy Museum of New Mexico.

3. *Sheep in Sandia or Manzano Mountain Pasture, ca. 1895. Dry land grazing took place on the sporadic rolling pasturage above the Rio Grande Valley.*
Courtesy Albuquerque Museum, Van Deren Coke Collection.

6. *Spanish weaving, carding and spinning at the Native Market in Santa Fe, New Mexico, ca. 1935. Not only did the Market provide a place for local artisans to work, it also acted as a retail outlet for textiles and other crafts made at the local vocational schools.*
Photo by T. Harmon Parkhurst.
Courtesy Museum of New Mexico.

8. *An unidentified woman weaves a rag rug at the WPA Project in Costilla, New Mexico, September 1939. Vocational projects, like this one at Costilla, encouraged a revival of Hispanic craft traditions in New Mexico in the 1930s.*
Photo by Russell Lee.
Courtesy Museum of New Mexico.

4. *Interior of the Indian Room at the Alvarado Hotel, Albuquerque, New Mexico, ca. 1905. Rio Grande and Navajo textiles, weaving tools and materials are displayed haphazardly, as if cultural identity were irrelevant.*
Courtesy Museum of New Mexico.

5. *Interior of the Kate Mueller residence, De Vargas Street, Santa Fe, New Mexico, ca. 1912. Photographs of home interiors from the early 1900s indicate a casual, eclectic mixing of Hispanic and Native American arts.*
Courtesy Museum of New Mexico.

PART TWO

INTRODUCTION TO THE CATALOGUE

TO FACILITATE CATALOGUING OF textiles in this collection, descriptive and analytical information from *Spanish Textile Tradition* was combined with Baizerman's "Textile Examination Record: Transitional Period Hispanic Weaving" and with the discussion in the preceding chapter of this publication. From these sources, a twelve-point system used to describe the Rio Grande blanket was developed and applied to each blanket in the collection.

1. DESIGN SYSTEM:

Each blanket is given a title indicating its period category (i.e., classic, transitional, Chimayo or revival) followed by the broad category "Rio Grande." Next the particular pattern is listed. And finally, textile use (i.e. blanket, furniture scarf, throw) is identified.[109]

2. DIMENSIONS:

Each blanket is measured in both meters and feet (in parentheses). First, the warp length is given. It includes the length of the fringe (when present). Second, the weft length, or blanket width, is listed. Beneath this measurement, the length of the fringe is noted in centimeters and inches (in parentheses). When fringe is present on one end only of the blanket, this is so noted.

3. PROBABLE DATE:

This is determined by the evaluation of all data available on the individual blanket included in each catalogue entry.

4. FABRIC STRUCTURE:

Fabric structure is described by two designations indicating first, the type of weave, and second, the weaving method used to achieve the width of the individual blanket.

Almost all Rio Grande blankets were weft-faced plain, balanced (rare) or tapestry weave (indicated in the first half of this description). As defined by Emery, a plain weave fabric contains "the simplest possible interlacing of warp and weft elements," that is over one and under one.[110] When the warp and weft elements are equally spaced and equal in flexibility and size, "the plain weave is described as balanced."[111] In contrast, a weft-faced fabric is one in which the "wefts are sufficiently numerous and sufficiently compacted to completely cover the warps."[112] Some Rio Grandes are weft-faced tapestry weaves, that is "weft-faced plain weave fabrics in which threads do not run from selvadge to selvadge but form the pattern, each one being woven back and forth over the warp threads where its particular color is needed."[113]

The desired width of a Rio Grande blanket is achieved in one of three ways. Blankets are said to be (**a**) single width, (**b**) single width, double-weave, or (**c**) double width with a center dovetailed seam (indicated in the second half of the description). Each of these was described in the preceding chapter of this study.

5. FIBER:

The particular type of fiber, or yarn, found in each blanket is listed, first for warp and then for weft. Most handspun warps found in Rio Grande blankets are 2-ply, ply indicating the number of strands of fiber twisted together in a length of yarn,[114] and Z-spun, indicating the directional twist employed in the spinning of the yarn.[115] When commercially spun fiber was used, it was most often 4-ply cotton twine.

Handspun wefts were 1-ply Z-spun fiber, usually wool. Commercial yarns were also used after mid-century. These are described individually under "Comments," when appropriate.

6. THREAD COUNT:

This indicates the warp-to-weft ratio per centimeter and per inch (in parentheses).

7. COLOR:

Color is listed in order of frequency. This is occasionally subjective, especially when there are four or more colors present. Most of the dye colors found in the collection are synthetic. Where natural color is identified, the color is preceded by the word "natural."

8. DESIGN MOTIF:

The individual pattern and detail found in each blanket are described according to the discussion presented in Chapter 4 of this study.

9. CONDITION:

All of the blankets in the collection are in good to excellent condition. Soiled spots, repair, broken warps, fugitive, that is, faded color, etc., are listed in order of importance.

10. COMPARABLE EXAMPLES:

Because most of the blankets in the collection are transitional, and few transitional blankets have been identified in publications or in museum records themselves, locating comparable examples was difficult. Comparable examples were selected from published rather than museum sources when available to facilitate comparison for the reader. The two main texts for comparison employed herein are *Spanish Textile Tradition* and *Weaving of the Southwest*. When published examples are unavailable, the reader is directed to appropriate museum collections.

11. PROVENANCE:

All of the blankets in this collection were collected by Mr. Will and the late Mrs. Liz Doty of Norman, Oklahoma, between 1975 and 1985. Most were purchased from private blanket dealers who wish to remain anonymous. Therefore, this point is omitted for all but one, blanket 3, in the collection where information was actually attached to the blanket itself.

12. COMMENTS:

In this section, observations of the writer and of weavers Jaramillo-Lavadie, Vergara Wilson and Ortega on individual blankets are described. Other comments include characteristics peculiar to the individual blanket and techniques mentioned in the design motif described above.

The blankets in this collection are grouped by design characteristics. Blankets 1–19 are simple striped or band and stripe examples. Blankets 20–23 are Saltillo-inspired patterns. Blankets 24–26 are Chimayo. And blanket 27 is a revival striped blanket. All of these were discussed in the greater context of Transitional Period Rio Grande blanketry in Chapter 4 of this study.

THE CATALOGUE

BLANKET 1

DESIGN SYSTEM:
Classic Rio Grande Five-Band Blanket.

DIMENSIONS:
1.14 X 1.17 m. (3'9" x 3'10").
Fringe: 2.2 cm. (7/8").

PROBABLE DATE:
Ca. 1850-1860.

FABRIC STRUCTURE:
Weft-faced plain weave; single width, double-weave.

FIBER:
Warp: 2-ply Z-spun handspun wool.
Weft: 1-ply Z-spun handspun wool.

THREAD COUNT:
3:9/cm. (8:26/in.).

COLOR:
Natural brown, blue (indigo?), natural white.

DESIGN MOTIF:
Wide bands of equal stripes of brown and blue with a center checkerboard blue and white stripe are separated by a narrow blue stripe flanked by narrow white stripes.

CONDITION:
Extensively repaired. Originally a five- or seven-band blanket, but the proportions of the fragment suggest the former. The worn center band was removed, and the two ends joined at the center where the cut warp ends were carefully worked up into the blanket.[116] Small holes were rewoven, and fringe was replaced. Frayed selvage edges were bound with well-matched synthetic yarns. This signature repair is also found in blankets 3 and 11.[117]

COMPARABLE EXAMPLES:
Plate 6, *Spanish Textile Tradition*, p. 61.

COMMENTS:
The checkerboard center stripe in each of the two remnant bands is characteristic of Rio Grande blankets. The checkerboard is "achieved by alternating light and dark weft shots [in this case blue and white] twice, then reversing to dark and light."[118] The process is repeated until the desired width of the stripe is achieved.

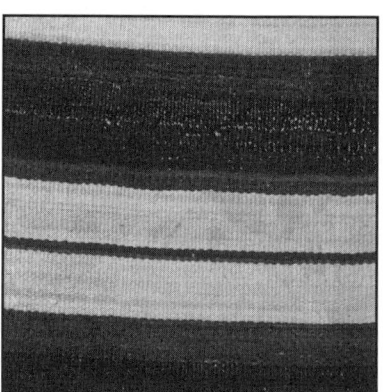

A FRAGMENT, this blanket was mended, perhaps, by a trader or collector who wished to increase the value of the blanket.

DETAIL

44

BLANKET 2

DESIGN SYSTEM:
Transitional Rio Grande Striped Blanket.

DIMENSIONS:
2.11 x 1.15 m. (6'11" x 3'9½").
Fringe: 3.8 cm. (1½").

PROBABLE DATE:
Ca. 1880.

FABRIC STRUCTURE:
Weft-faced plain weave;
single width, double-weave.

FIBER:
Warp: 2-ply Z-spun handspun wool.
Weft: 1-ply Z-spun handspun wool.

THREAD COUNT:
2:9/cm. (6:23/in.).

COLOR:
Natural white, natural grey, pink, natural brown.

DESIGN MOTIF:
Roughly even ticked stripes not arranged in bands.

CONDITION:
Scattered unrepaired small holes.
Fugitive orange, pink.

COMPARABLE EXAMPLES:
Plate 11, *Spanish Textile Tradition*, p. 68.

COMMENTS:
Unbanded stripe patterns were common, employed especially in the transitional period when design systems began to break down. In this example, the stripes, which would otherwise be monotonous due to their even rhythm, were made interesting by the use of repeated ticking. The procedure is identical to that of the checkerboard, except that in this pattern, the weft shots are only repeated twice, to create a dentate-like edge on individual stripes.[119]

DETAIL

WEFT SHOTS of dark and light yarn were alternated to create a dentate-like edge on each stripe. The process is similar to checkerboard patterning.

BLANKET 3

DESIGN SYSTEM:
Transitional Rio Grande Five-Band Blanket.

DIMENSIONS:
2.16 x 1.23 m. (7'1" x 4½").
Fringe: 2.5 cm. (1").

PROBABLE DATE:
Ca. 1860-1880.

FABRIC STRUCTURE:
Weft-faced plain weave; double width, center dovetailed seam.

FIBER:
Warp: 2-ply Z-spun handspun wool.
Weft: 1-ply Z-spun handspun wool.

THREAD COUNT:
3:13/cm. (8:30/in.).

COLOR:
Natural dark brown (probably young *churro*), natural white, yellow, purple, salmon, orange, green.

DESIGN MOTIF:
Five-band system composed of narrow even stripes with some ticking.

CONDITION:
Large repaired section. Dull areas of repair in carefully matched yarns. Cotton repair warps.

COMPARABLE EXAMPLES:
Blanket #5069, the Taylor Museum, Colorado Springs, Colorado.

PROVENANCE:
Attached label:
"M. S. Deitrich, 519 Canyon Road."

COMMENTS:
Margretta Stewart Dietrich (1881-1961) moved to Santa Fe in 1927. She purchased her home, *El Zaguán*, at 519 Canyon Road sometime between 1927 and 1931. She began collecting local arts and crafts almost immediately. Locals sold handmade objects, perhaps such as this blanket, to her on a regular basis.[120] It was a practice among Santa Fe art collectors to hire locals to repair broken or worn artifacts.[121] It is possible that she hired the weaver who rewove this blanket. Similarities to repairs made in blankets 1 and 11 suggest that these, too, were rewoven by the same hand. A second possibility is that these three blankets were repaired by a trader who wished to increase the value and visual appeal of the textiles.[122]

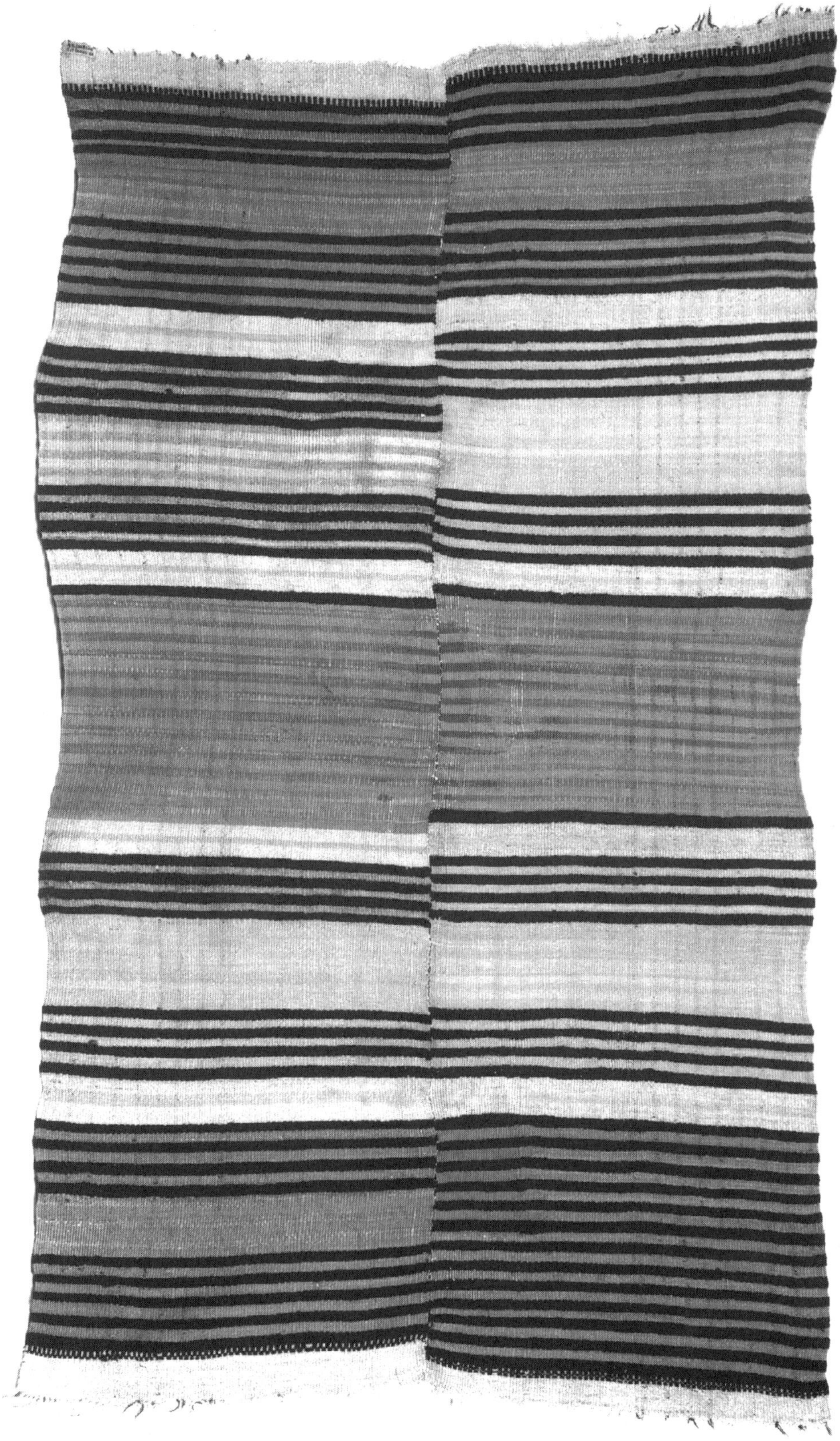

BLANKET 4

DESIGN SYSTEM:
Transitional Rio Grande Band and Stripe Blanket.

DIMENSIONS:
2.21 x 1.5 m. (7'3" x 3'9").
Fringe: 3.8 cm. (1½").

PROBABLE DATE:
Ca. 1880-1900.

FABRIC STRUCTURE:
Weft-faced plain weave;
single width, double-weave.

FIBER:
Warp: 2-ply Z-spun handspun wool.
Weft: 1-ply Z-spun handspun wool.

THREAD COUNT
3:16/cm. (8:42/in.).

COLOR:
Natural white, red, purple, yellow-orange.

DESIGN MOTIF:
Variegated stripes with some ticking in five wide bands.
In this example, the bands are difficult to discern, but
each contains a distinct wide center stripe.

CONDITION:
Good. Broken wool warps repaired with commercial
cotton twine. Fugitive purple, red, yellow-orange.

COMPARABLE EXAMPLES:
None.

COMMENTS:
The uneven quality of the warp yarns, probably
responsible for the warp breakage, suggests that this
blanket was woven on an old hand-hewn loom, therefore
its anticipated date of production would be mid-century.
The high warp-to-weft ratio, however, indicates
a post-1880 date. The use of synthetic dyes also
indicates a later production date. Commercial cotton
twine was used to repair broken warps.
As noted, commercial cotton twine was available in
quantity after 1880. It was a material popular for
use in warp repair.[123]

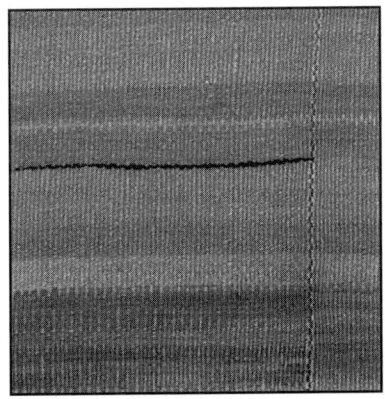

DETAIL

*THIS ACCIDENTAL dark shot of yarn
was perhaps a remnant, caught
up in the yarn prepared by the weaver.*

BLANKET 5

DESIGN SYSTEM:
Transitional Rio Grande Five-Band Blanket.

DIMENSIONS:
1.92 x 1.14 m. (7'4½" x 3'9¼").
Fringe: 3.8 cm. (1½"), one end only.

PROBABLE DATE:
Ca. 1880-1900.

FABRIC STRUCTURE:
Weft-faced plain weave; double width, center dovetailed seam.

FIBER:
Warp: 4-ply commercial cotton twine.
Weft: 1 ply Z-spun handspun wool.

THREAD COUNT:
4:14/cm. (10:34/in.).

COLOR:
Medium natural brown (pure, young *churro*), natural dark brown, natural white, red.

DESIGN MOTIF:
Five equal bands of white, dark brown, and red and white checkerboard stripes, on a wide medium brown background.

CONDITION:
Excellent.
Slightly fugitive synthetic red.
Minimal careful repair of broken warps. Some wear on vertical selvages.

COMPARABLE EXAMPLES:
Fig. 1, *Spanish Textile Tradition*, p. 58.
In this example, six equal bands of natural white and natural brown stripes float on a wide background of natural medium brown.

COMMENTS:
The soft texture, or "hand", the subtle color variation, and the lustrous sheen of the background yarns indicate that these yarns are pure *churro*. Moreover, the richness and depth of color in this area point to a young animal as the source of the wool.[124] This could suggest a mid-century date. However, the presence of cotton warp and synthetic red dye date the blanket to post-1880, but probably no later than 1890 because of the purity of the background wool.

BLANKET 6

DESIGN SYSTEM:
Transitional Rio Grande Five-Band Blanket.

DIMENSIONS:
1.82 x .86 m. (5'11½" x 2'10").
Fringe: 2.5 cm. (1").

PROBABLE DATE:
Ca. 1870-1880.

FABRIC STRUCTURE:
Weft-faced plain weave; double width, center dovetailed seam.

FIBER:
Warp: 2-ply Z-spun handspun wool.
Weft: 1-ply Z-spun handspun wool.

THREAD COUNT:
3:8/cm. (8:20/in.).

COLOR:
Turquoise, hot pink, gold, burgundy, purple.

DESIGN MOTIF:
Five wide bands of near-solid color separated by even purple and hot pink stripes. May also be read as six bands of stripes on near-solid backgrounds of gold and burgundy.

CONDITION:
Repaired selvages and holes. Fugitive pink and purple.

COMPARABLE EXPAMPLES:
Plate 6, *Weaving of the Southwest*, p. 60.

COMMENTS:
This example probably relates to the *jerga* runner, a woven fabric used primarily for floor covering. The narrow and uneven quality of the right half of the blanket compared to the slightly wider and more finely woven left half indicate that the two halves were woven on different looms, perhaps by different weavers of unequal skill. However, the consistency of the colors, the patterns and spin of the yarns suggest that the two halves were woven in the same household. It is probable that these two halves were originally part of a long narrow *jerga*-like runner which was cut down. The remnant pieces were then resown with a center seam.

BLANKET 7

DESIGN SYSTEM:
Transitional Rio Grande Striped Blanket.

DIMENSIONS:
1.78 x 1.33 m. (5'10" x 4'4½").
Fringe: None.

PROBABLE DATE:
Ca. 1880-1900.

FABRIC STRUCTURE:
Weft-faced plain weave; single width, double-weave.

FIBER:
Warp: 4-ply commercial cotton twine.
Weft: 1-ply Z-spun handspun wool.

THREAD COUNT:
3:8/cm. (6:20/in.).

COLOR:
Orange, green, black, red, natural white.

DESIGN MOTIF:
Narrow bands of even orange and green stripes alternate with narrow bands of red and black stripes with a center stripe composed of black and white columns. The very narrow central stripe is beaded, a pattern made by alternating weft shots of black and natural white.

CONDITION:
Center hole repaired. Some small soiled spots. Broken warps. Fugitive orange, green, black.

COMPARABLE EXAMPLES:
Vertical columns appear in Plate 116, *Weaving of the Southwest*, p.48.

COMMENTS:
The vertical column is yet another variation on the checkerboard theme.

BLANKET 8

DESIGN SYSTEM:
Transitional Rio Grande Striped Blanket.

DIMENSIONS:
2.28 x 1.24 m. (7'6" x 4'1").
Fringe: 6.4 cm. (2½").

PROBABLE DATE:
Ca. 1880-1900.

FABRIC STRUCTURE:
Weft-faced plain weave; double width, center dovetailed seam.

FIBER:
Warp: 4-ply commercial cotton twine.
Weft: 1-ply Z-spun handspun wool.

THREAD COUNT
4:13/cm. (10:30/in.)

COLOR:
Natural white, green, salmon, pink, purple (on dark wool).

DESIGN MOTIF:
Irregular, asymmetrical stripes.

CONDITION:
Minimal moth damage. Worn selvage.
Fugitive green, pink, purple.

COMPARABLE EXAMPLES
None.

COMMENTS:
Interpretation of this blanket is problematic. The assymetrical, unplanned quality of the pattern suggests that this blanket might have been intended for utilitarian usage. And the occasional mismatching of the pattern suggests an unskilled hand. However, the fineness of the weave which produced a smooth, even texture indicates the hand of a highly skilled weaver.

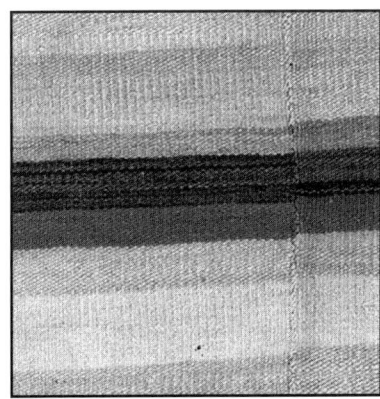

DETAIL

***THE FINE TEXTURE** of this blanket indicates the hand of a highly skilled weaver.*

BLANKET 9

DESIGN SYSTEM:
Transitional Rio Grande Five-Band Blanket.

DIMENSIONS:
2.22 x 1.34 m. (7'3" x 4'4½").
Fringe: None.

PROBABLE DATE:
Ca. 1880-1900.

FABRIC STRUCTURE:
Weft-faced plain weave; single width, double-weave.

FIBER:
Warp: 4-ply commercial cotton twine.
Weft: 1-ply Z-spun handspun wool.

THREAD COUNT:
3:6/cm. (6:16/in.).

COLOR:
Burgundy, orange, green, pink.

DESIGN MOTIF:
Five narrow striped bands on a wide burgundy background.

CONDITION:
Excellent. Several small soiled spots.

COMPARABLE EXAMPLES:
The predominant burgundy background in this example relates it to the predominantly red blanket in Plate 12, *Spanish Textile Tradition*, p. 69.

COMMENTS:
To Jaramillo-Lavadie, the unusually tightly beaten weft and tight double center warps, requiring great strength, suggest a male weaver.[125] Rio Grande blankets produced for home consumption were intended for use in a dimly lit, earthen interior. The rich, deep red of this blanket, made possible by synthetic dyes, would have been much appreciated in such an environment. Red was an especially popular color toward the end of the 1800s.

BLANKET 10

DESIGN SYSTEM:
Transitional Rio Grande Striped Blanket.

DIMENSIONS:
1.99 x 1.29 m. (6'6½" x 4'3").
Fringe: 3.8 cm. (1½").

PROBABLE DATE:
Ca. 1860-1880.

FABRIC STRUCTURE:
Weft-faced plain weave; double width, center dovetailed seam.

FIBER:
Warp: 2-ply Z-spun handspun wool.
Weft: 1-ply Z-spun handspun wool.

THREAD COUNT:
3:13/cm. (8:30/in.).

COLOR:
Natural white, natural dark brown, green, pink, purple.

DESIGN MOTIF:
Even narrow bands of pink, green and purple stripes on a white background. Wide center stripe of alternating brown and pink vertical columns.

CONDITION:
Carefully repaired small holes. Small soiled spots. Broken warps. Fugitive green, pink, purple.

COMPARABLE EXAMPLES:
Compare with blanket 12, p. 55.

COMMENTS:
Frayed and broken warps suggest the use of an old loom built of hand-adzed, unmilled lumber.

BLANKET 11

DESIGN SYSTEM:
Transitional Rio Grande Striped Blanket.

DIMENSIONS:
1.90 x 1.05 m. (6'½" x 3'5½").
Fringe: 6.3 cm. (2½").

PROBABLE DATE:
Ca. 1880-1900

FABRIC STRUCTURE:
Weft-faced plain weave; double width, center dovetailed seam.

FIBER:
Warp: 4-ply commercial cotton twine.
Weft: 1-ply Z-spun handspun wool.

THREAD COUNT:
3:10/cm. (8:22/in.).

COLOR:
Blue, natural brown, pink, natural white, red.

DESIGN MOTIF:
Bands of wide, even, ticked stripes.
Center band of narrow stripes.

CONDITION:
Repaired holes. Repaired vertical selvages.
Fugitive blue, pink, red.

COMPARABLE EXAMPLES:
None.

COMMENTS:
The upper right corner of this blanket demonstrates perfectly the fugitive and temporal nature of synthetic dyes of the period, possibly due to the inexperience of the weaver with the new technique. The weaver perhaps ran out of the natural brown yarn used in the bulk of the blanket. He/she replaced it with a synthetic-dyed handspun wool, originally a deep purple, now faded. In the dimly lit interior of a late nineteenth-century Hispanic home, the deep purple and the dark brown would have seemed, perhaps, almost identical in color.

BLANKET 12

DESIGN SYSTEM:
Transitional Rio Grande Striped Blanket.

DIMENSIONS:
1.73 x 1.13 m. (5'8" x 3'8½").
Fringe: 5 cm. (2").

PROBABLE DATE:
Ca. 1880-1900.

FABRIC STRUCTURE:
Weft-faced plain weave; double width, center dovetailed seam.

FIBER:
Warp: 4-ply commercial cotton twine.
Weft: 1-ply Z-spun handspun wool.

THREAD COUNT:
4:7/cm. (10:18/in.).

COLOR:
Natural white, natural dark brown, green, pink.

DESIGN MOTIF:
Even stripes of each color. Center stripe of alternating dark brown and white columns.

CONDITION:
Excellent. Slightly worn vertical selvage. Fugitive green and pink.

COMPARABLE EXAMPLES:
See blanket 10, p. 53. No comparable design examples have been found outside of the collection, but both blankets fill all other Rio Grande blanket criteria.

COMMENTS:
The rich, redish tonality of the dark brown yarn suggests that it is predominantly *churro*. The consistently fine quality of the spin of the yarn is unusual in what was probably considered a utilitarian blanket.[126]

BLANKET 13

DESIGN SYSTEM:
Transitional Rio Grande Nine-Band Blanket.

DIMENSIONS:
2.40 x 1.32 m. (7'10½" x 4'4¼").
Fringe: 7.5 cm. (3").

PROBABLE DATE:
Ca. 1880-1900.

FABRIC STRUCTURE:
Weft-faced plain weave; double width, center dovetailed seam.

FIBER:
Warp: 4-ply commercial cotton twine.
Weft: 1-ply Z-spun handspun wool.

THREAD COUNT:
3:15/cm. (8:34/in.).

COLOR:
Natural white, purple, pink, natural brown, orange.

DESIGN MOTIF:
Nine bands of even stripes on white ground. Narrow center orange and brown beaded stripe.

CONDITION:
Excellent. Small scattered stains. Fugitive pink, purple.

COMPARABLE EXAMPLES:
Beading is visible in Plate 4, *Spanish Textile Tradition*, p. 60.

COMMENTS:
The traditional five- or seven-band system was modified in the transitional period to include patterns of nine or even eleven bands. In this example, bands of purple and pink alternate with bands of orange and brown. When this blanket was first woven and fading of the fugitive purple and pink had not yet occurred, this blanket must have vibrated with intense color. Ticking would not have been needed to relieve the monotony of the even striping. The beading in the center stripe was achieved by alternating weft shots of orange and brown.

BLANKET 14

DESIGN SYSTEM:
Transitional Rio Grande Five-Band Blanket.

DIMENSIONS:
2.22 x 1.37 (7'3½" x 4'6").
Fringe: None.

PROBABLE DATE:
Ca. 1880-1900.

FABRIC STRUCTURE:
Weft-faced plain weave;
single width, double-weave.

FIBER:
Warp: 4-ply commercial cotton twine.
Weft: 1-ply Z-spun handspun cotton.

THREAD COUNT:
3:9/cm. (6:20/in.).

COLOR:
Natural brown, red, natural white, pink, orange.

DESIGN MOTIF:
Five bands of narrow stripes separated by
wide stripes of natural brown.

CONDITION:
Repaired warps. Worn
horizontal selvage. Fugitive pink.

COMPARABLE EXAMPLES:
The evenness of the five bands and their proportional
relationship to the natural brown stripes is
similar to that found in
Plate 4, *Spanish Textile Tradition*, p. 60.

COMMENTS:
In this blanket, as in so many others, the
outside warps on either vertical selvage are doubled to
increase the strength at this vulnerable spot.

BLANKET 15

DESIGN SYSTEM:
Transitional Rio Grande Band and Stripe Blanket.

DIMENSIONS:
2.37 x 1.22 m. (7'9½" x 4'1¼").
Fringe: None.

PROBABLE DATE:
Ca. 1890-1910.

FABRIC STRUCTURE:
Weft-faced plain weave; single width.

FIBER:
Warp: 4-ply commercial cotton twine.
Weft: 1-ply Z-spun handspun wool.

THREAD COUNT:
3:13 cm. (7:29/in.).

COLOR:
Red, yellow, natural white, purple.

DESIGN MOTIF:
Nine bands of white and yellow stripes on a red background banded by narrow purple ticking.

CONDITION:
Good. Frayed selvages. Some soiled spots. Fugitive purple which has bled into white.

COMPARABLE EXAMPLES:
Band to background relationship is similar to that found in Plate 112, *Weaving of the Southwest*, p. 45.

COMMENTS:
This blanket is single width without a double center warp, indicating that it was woven on a wider loom, perhaps one introduced to Chimayo by J. S. Candelario, a Santa Fe dealer, in 1890.[127]

BLANKET 16

DESIGN SYSTEM:
Transitional Rio Grande Five-Band Blanket.

DIMENSIONS:
1.87 x 1.35 m. (6'1½" x 4'5").
Fringe: 3.8 cm. (1.5"), one end only.

PROBABLE DATE:
Ca. 1880-1900.

FABRIC STRUCTURE:
Weft-faced plain weave;
double width, center dovetailed seam.

FIBER:
Warp: 4-ply commercial cotton twine.
Weft: 1-ply Z-spun handspun wool
with some angora mohair.

THREAD COUNT:
3:7/cm. (6:16/in.).

COLOR:
Red, blue-green, yellow, dark blue.

DESIGN MOTIF:
Five bands of even stripes on a red background.

CONDITION:
Excellent. Scattered soiled spots. Occasional pulled warps, that is, some warps are off vertical alignment because of the tightness of the weft yarns. Fugitive yellow.

COMPARABLE EXAMPLES:
None.

COMMENTS:
The red and blue-green yarns in this example are partially composed of mohair from the angora goat (Blanket 22).[128] The angora has long (4"-10") luxurious hair rather than oily wool. Angora has no felting properties, therefore it is difficult to spin,[129] perhaps one of the reasons for its scarcity in Rio Grande weaving. No studies on the angora in colonial New Mexico have as yet been undertaken, but the goat is listed among the animals brought with Oñate and others.[130] The angora was excluded, however, from communal grazing in New Mexico in 1915.[131] This suggests that the angora population was on the rise just after the turn of the century. Characteristically, the warp ends on a Rio Grande blanket were cut from the loom and knotted in groups of three or more to create a fringe of variable length.[132]

BLANKET 17

DESIGN SYSTEM:
Transitional Rio Grande Striped Blanket.

DIMENSIONS:
2.18 x 1.33 (7'2" x 4'5").
Fringe: None.

PROBABLE DATE:
Ca. 1880-1890.

FABRIC STRUCTURE:
Weft-faced plain weave;
single width, double-weave.

FIBER:
Warp: 4-ply commercial cotton twine.
Weft: 1-ply Z-spun handspun wool.

THREAD COUNT:
3:4/cm. (6:10/in.).

COLOR:
Natural white, natural dark brown.

DESIGN MOTIF:
Asymmetrical natural dark brown stripes, some
composed of alternating brown and
white columns, on a natural white background.

CONDITION:
Excellent.

COMPARABLE EXAMPLES:
None.

COMMENTS:
Although the asymmetrical quality of the pattern is
not typical of Rio Grande textiles, all other criteria
are met in this blanket, thus the identification.
To the modern weaver, this blanket suggests
a meditation piece. The occassional asymmetrical
brown stripe is both a marker in the
length of the textile, as well as a means
to avoid boredom.[133]

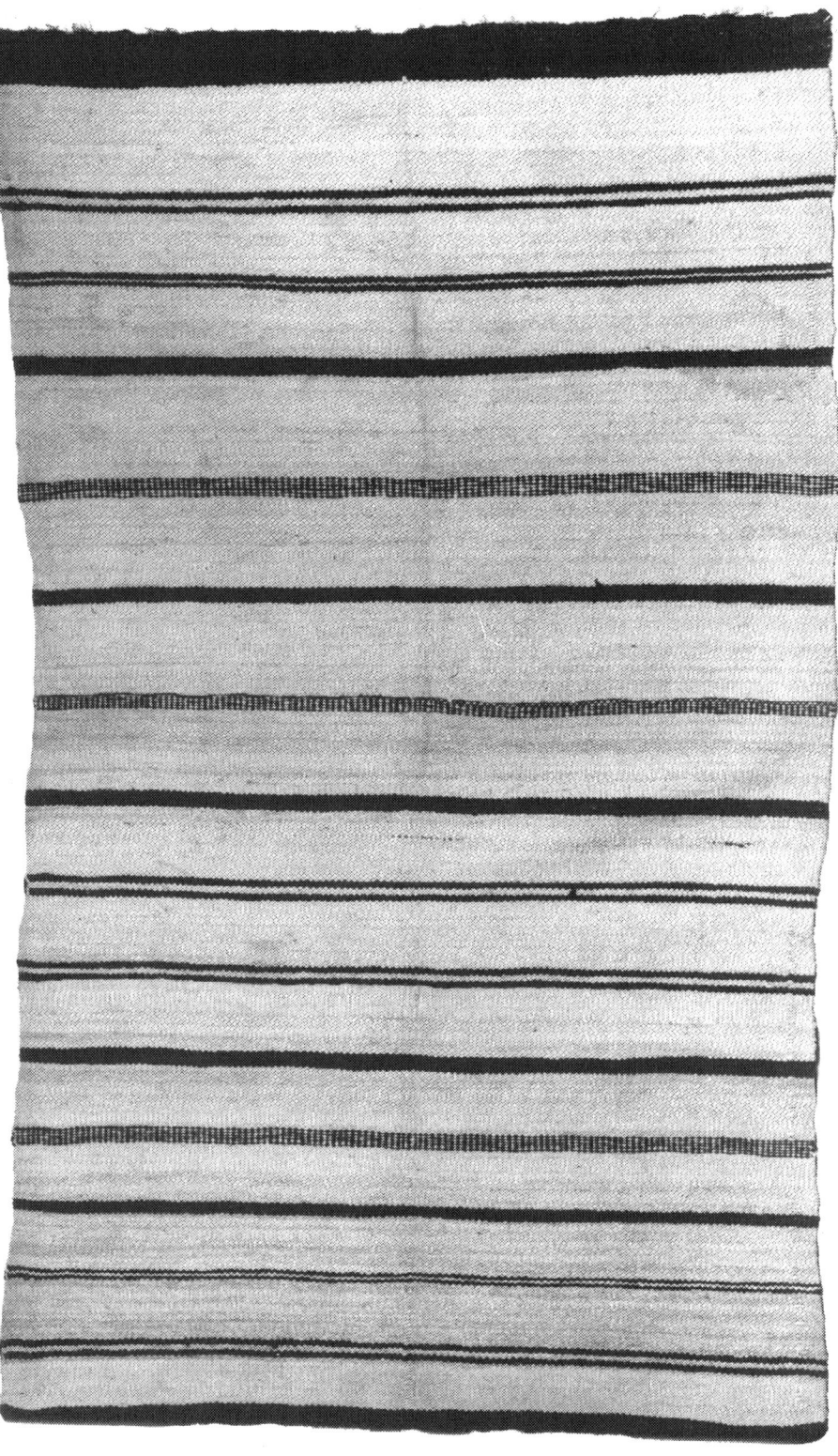

BLANKET 18

DESIGN SYSTEM:
Transitional Rio Grande Striped Blanket.

DIMENSIONS:
2.16 x 1.30 m. (7'1" x 4'3").
Fringe: None.

PROBABLE DATE:
Ca. 1880-1900.

FABRIC STRUCTURE:
Weft-faced plain weave; double width, center seam, not dovetailed.

FIBER:
Warp: 4-ply commercial cotton twine.
Weft: 1-ply Z-spun handspun wool.

THREAD COUNT:
3-4:10/cm. (8-10:24/in.).

COLOR:
Natural white, blue, red, orange, pink, yellow.

DESIGN MOTIF:
Even stripes of solid color without a regular color pattern.

CONDITION:
Broken warps. Worn selvages.
Fugitive pink, yellow.

COMPARABLE EXAMPLES:
None.

COMMENTS:
Because of the presence of various weights and qualities of warp yarns employed in this blanket, as well as the uneven skill of the weaver, or weavers, this blanket might have been a teaching tool. On first inspection, this weaving might be considered utilitairan due to the uneven quality of the weave. But then, its relative excellent condition could be questioned. When queried, Jaramillo-Lavadie suggested it might have been a spinning sampler, one in which all family members participated.[134]
If this were the case, then the blanket would have possibly been considered part of the family heritage, and revered as such.

61

BLANKET 19

DESIGN SYSTEM:
Transitional Rio Grande Six-Band Blanket.

DIMENSIONS:
2.36 x 1.38 m. (7'9" x 4'6½").
Fringe: 5 cm. (2"), one end only.

PROBABLE DATE:
Ca. 1910-1920.

FABRIC STRUCTURE:
Weft-faced plain weave;
double width, center dovetailed seam.

FIBER:
Warp: 4-ply commercial pastel cotton twine.
Weft: 1-ply Z-spun handspun wool.

THREAD COUNT:
2-3:13/cm. (6:32/in.).

COLOR:
Natural white, red, natural (?) green on
a strong yellow mordant (color fixer).

DESIGN MOTIF:
Six equal bands of even red and green stripes
on a white background. Some ticking.

CONDITION:
Good. Some small holes at center seam.
Large, yellow soiled spots. Fugitive green.

COMPARABLE EXAMPLES:
None.

COMMENTS:
It is possible that the faded green is a
natural color. It was dyed over a clearly visible strong
yellow mordant, a process typical in the use of natural
colors.[135] Jaramillo-Lavadie suggested this blanket
was woven after 1900 because of the
coarseness of the spin. Also, the use of multi-colored
pastel cotton warp is datable to
1910 through 1930.[136]

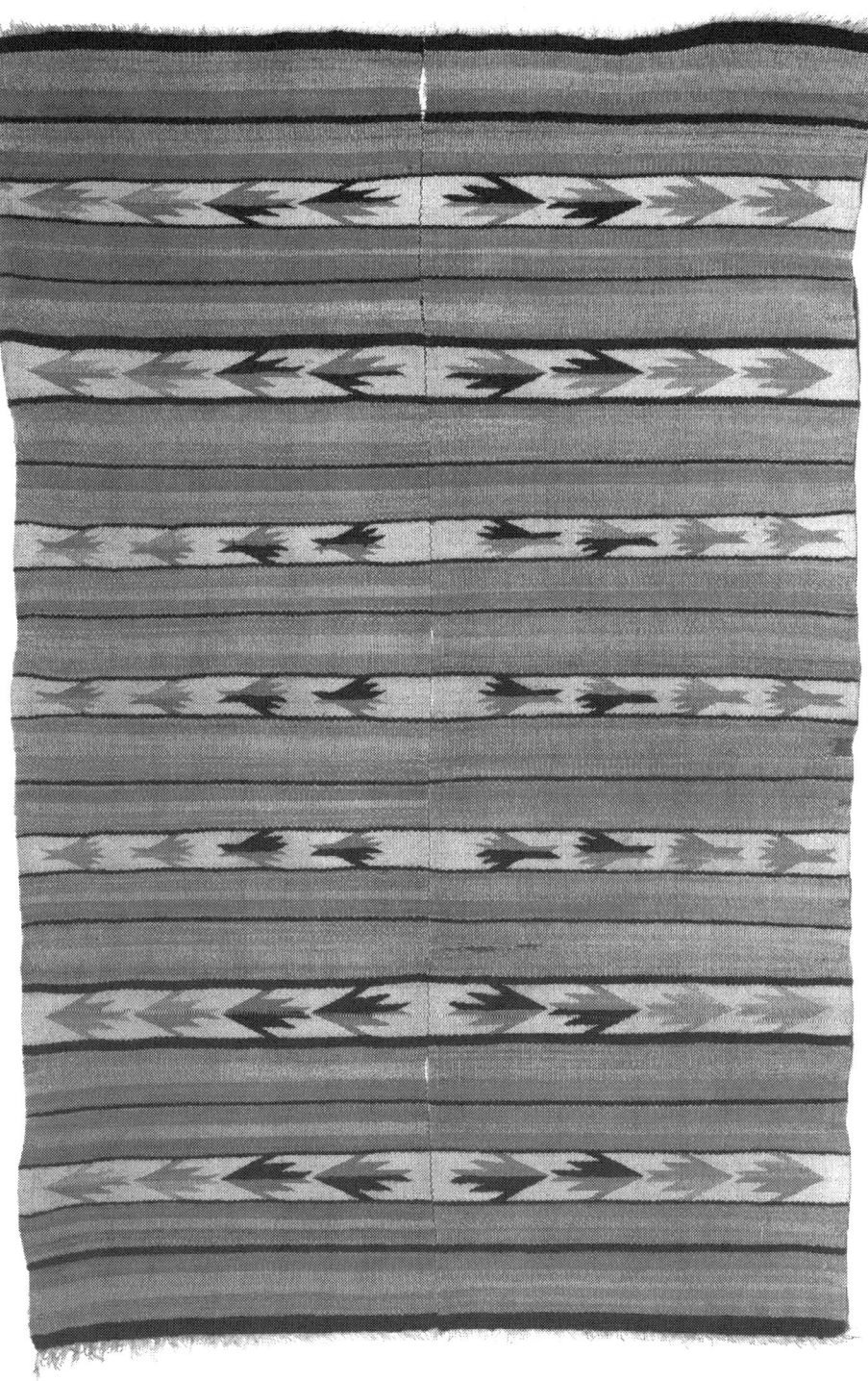

BLANKET 20

DESIGN SYSTEM:
Transitional Rio Grande Seven-Band Blanket with Saltillo Design Elements.

DIMENSIONS:
1.88 x 1.22 m. (6'2" x 4'½").
Fringe: 2.5 cm. (1").

PROBABLE DATE:
Ca. 1870-1880.

FABRIC STRUCTURE:
Weft-faced plain and tapestry weave; double width, center dovetailed seam.

FIBER:
Warp: 2-ply Z-spun handspun wool.
Weft: 1-ply Z-spun handspun wool.

THREAD COUNT:
3:12-13/cm. (7:28/in.).

COLOR:
Red, green, natural white, orange, natural brown, purple.

DESIGN MOTIF:
Seven-band with Saltillo *palmitas* (some stemmed with an "open beak") in the center stripe of each band. The *palmitas* are reversed from one half of the blanket to the other, creating a mirror image.

CONDITION:
Excellent. Minimal selvage repair. Fugitive red and green.

COMPARABLE EXAMPLES:
Rows of single leaves in the center stripe of each band recall a similar pattern found in Fig. 5, *Spanish Textile Tradition*, p. 93.

COMMENTS:
This blanket is an excellent example of the design system. The presence of the stemmed *palmita* with an open beak is unusual. No other blankets of this type examined contain this particular variant.

BLANKET 21

DESIGN SYSTEM:
Transitional Rio Grande Saltillo-Style Sampler.

DIMENSIONS:
.71 x .69 m. (2'4" x 2'3").
Fringe: None.

PROBABLE DATE:
Ca. 1880-1900.

FABRIC STRUCTURE:
Weft-faced tapestry and plain weave; single width.

FIBER:
Warp: 4-ply commercial cotton twine.
Weft: 1-ply Z-spun handspun wool.

THREAD COUNT:
2-3:5/cm. (6:12/in.).

COLOR:
Indigo (?), natural white, red.

DESIGN MOTIF:
Central serrate radiating diamond on an indigo background. White serrate vertical selvage borders. Narrow horizontal selvage bands of red and white stripes.

CONDITION:
Good. Frayed horizontal selvage borders. Fugitive red.

COMPARABLE EXAMPLES:
None.

COMMENTS:
The design system in this blanket was borrowed from the Saltillo *sarape*, but the pattern is clearly simplified. Its small size and the apparent lack of skill of the weaver suggest that this was perhaps a child's sampler or beginner's piece.

BLANKET 22

DESIGN SYSTEM:
Transitional Rio Grande Saltillo-Style Blanket.

DIMENSIONS:
2.05 x 1.41 m. (6'9" x 4'7½").
Fringe: 3.8 cm. (1½").

PROBABLE DATE:
Ca. 1870-1880.

FABRIC STRUCTURE:
Weft-faced tapestry and plain weave;
double width, center dovetailed seam.

FIBER:
Warp: 2-ply Z-spun handspun wool.
Weft: 1-ply Z-spun handspun wool.

THREAD COUNT:
3:10-11/cm. (6:24/in.).

COLOR:
Green, red, natural white,
natural brown, pink, yellow.

DESIGN MOTIF:
Radiating serrate center diamond elaborated
by serrate chevrons. Framed on the vertical selvages by
an elaborate Vallero-style border composed of vertical
rows of interlocking serrate diamonds.
Bands of narrow stripes across the horizontal
selvages complete the frame.

CONDITION:
Excellent. Some small, scattered, soiled spots.
Fugitive green, pink, yellow.

COMPARABLE EXAMPLES:
The radiating serrate center diamond recalls similar
ones in Figs. 5 and 6, *Spanish Textile Tradition*, p. 119.
The serrate chevrons which frame the central
motif relate to a similar device in Plate 50, *Spanish
Textile Tradition*, p. 116. The vertical rows of
interlocking serrate diamonds of the side borders
resemble the background motif in Plate 38,
Spanish Textile Tradition, p. 108.

COMMENTS:
Vergara Wilson called this example
a "blanket-within-a-blanket." The Eyedazzler-like
center reads as a separate blanket which
floats above the vertical borders.[137]

**SERRATED EDGES
are typical of Saltillo-
Style Rio Grande
Blankets.**

DETAIL

BLANKET 23

DESIGN SYSTEM:
Revival Saltillo-Style Blanket.

DIMENSIONS:
2.04 x 1.33 m. (6'8" x 4'4½").
Fringe: 5 cm. (2").

PROBABLE DATE:
Ca. 1930s.

FABRIC STRUCTURE:
Weft-faced tapestry and plain weave;
single width.

FIBER:
Warp: 3-ply commercial cotton twine.
Weft: 1-ply Z-spun commercial wool.

THREAD COUNT:
5:18-19/cm. (12:42/in.).

COLOR:
Turquoise blue, natural white,
salmon, dark brown, gold.

DESIGN MOTIF:
Radiating serrate center diamond on a background of vertical interlocking serrate diamonds. Vertical selvage frame composed of diagonal rows of serrate diamonds. Band of narrow stripes frame the blanket on the horizontal selvages.

CONDITION:
Excellent.

COMPARABLE EXAMPLES:
The floating, self-contained center diamond anchored by a dark vertical stripe on a background of vertical stripes composed of interlocking diamonds recalls the pattern found in Plate 40, *Spanish Textile Tradition*, p. 108. The vertical selvage framing device resembles that in Plate 39, *Spanish Textile Tradition*, p. 109.

COMMENTS:
The use of the wide loom, the presence of 3-ply cotton warp and the high thread count all suggest post-1900 production. The presence of the odd turquoise blue commercial yarn is problematic. The color was usually associated with a natural-dyed, handspun yarn referred to as "Native Market blue." Perhaps the weaver, aware of Native Market revival blankets, attempted to achieve similar effects with commercial yarns.[138]

BLANKET 24

DESIGN SYSTEM:
Early Chimayo Furniture Scarf.

DIMENSIONS:
2.21 x .71 m. (7'3" x 2'4").
Fringe: None.

PROBABLE DATE:
Ca. 1880-1885.

FABRIC STRUCTURE:
Weft-faced tapestry weave; single width.

FIBER:
Warp: 4-ply commercial cotton twine.
Weft: 3-ply Early Germantown wool.

THREAD COUNT:
5:16/cm. (12:36/in.).

COLOR:
Deep red, natural white, purple, green.

DESIGN MOTIF:
Central Navajo four-wind walking pattern,
or "Swastika," on a deep red background.
Background patterns composed of border vertical
rows of large, independent serrate chevrons
which flank a central vertical
row of independent serrate diamonds.

CONDITION:
Excellent. Fugitive red in the center area
only, indicating different dye vats.

COMPARABLE EXAMPLES:
The walking-four-wind pattern
is found in Plates 232-34,
Weaving of the Southwest, p. 94.

COMMENTS:
The use of the walking four-wind pattern has its
source in Navajo imagery. The color palette and the
use of 3-ply Early Germantown yarn suggest
pre-1880 production. The furniture scarf
was designed for the tourist market sometime
after 1880.[139] Therefore, this
textile probably dates to ca. 1880-85.

BLANKET 25

DESIGN SYSTEM:
Early Chimayo Blanket.

DIMENSIONS:
1.70 x 1.21 m. (5'3 x 3'11½").
Fringe: None.

PROBABLE DATE:
Ca. 1890-1900.

FABRIC STRUCTURE:
Weft-faced tapestry weave; single width.

FIBER:
Warp: 4-ply commercial cotton twine.
Weft: 3-ply synthetic-dyed Clasgens wool.

THREAD COUNT:
4:13/cm (9:30/in.).

COLOR:
Red, black, natural white, green.

DESIGN MOTIF:
Central serrate diamond, repeated in simplified form at four corners. Entire central motif enclosed in a black and white hourglass and chevron "chain."

CONDITION:
Excellent. Fading on one side only.

COMPARABLE EXAMPLES:
None.

COMMENTS:
This blanket was provided at a later date with a purple satin sleeve through which a dowel was passed. The blanket was then used as a wall hanging, apparently for quite some time, judging from the amount of fading visible on one side only. When shown this blanket, David Ortega, of Chimayo, identified it as a family competition piece, a symbol of the virtuosity of the weaver. He said, "we [the family] are very competitive among ourselves." He also identified the commercial yarn as Clasgens, about which little has been written.[140]

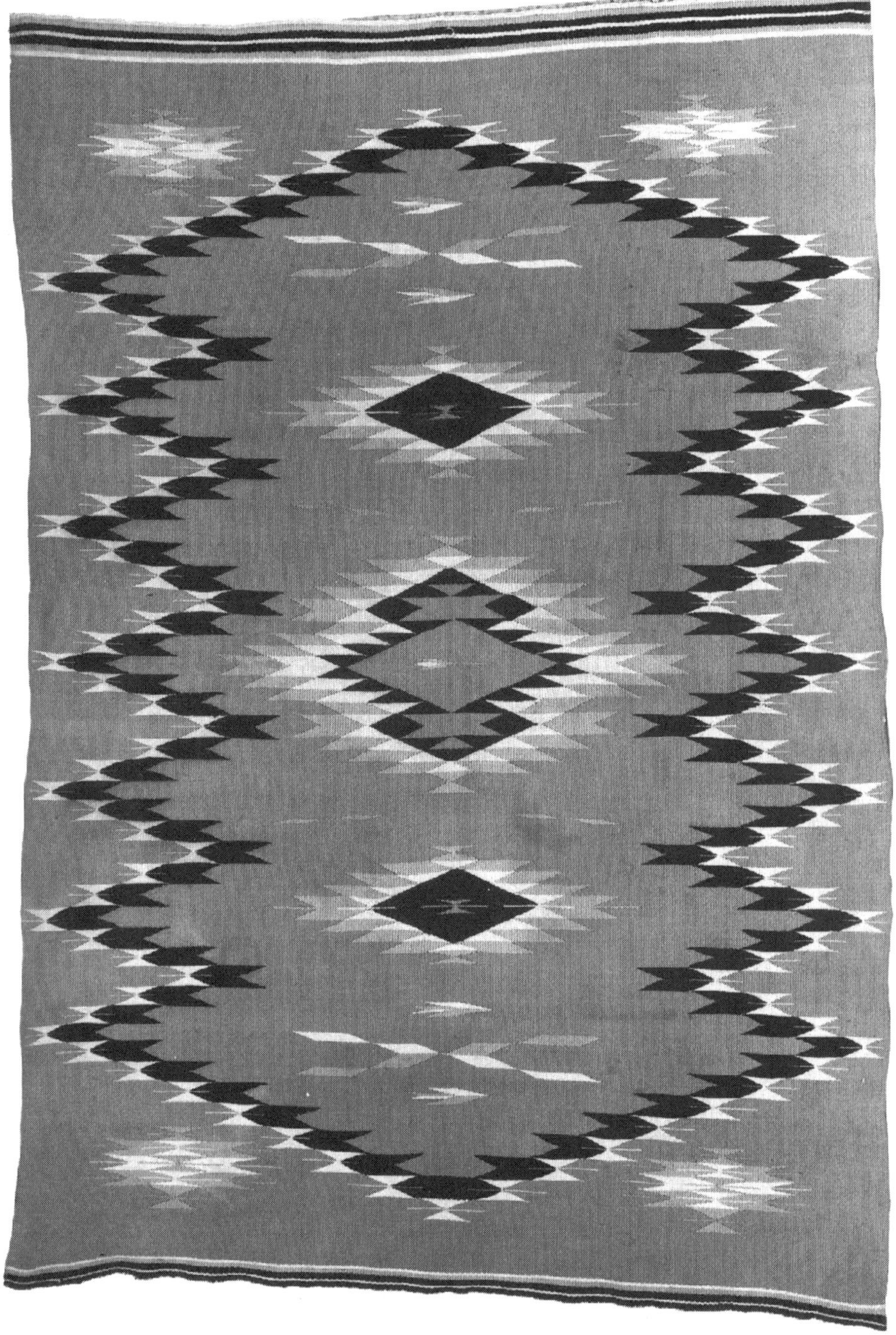

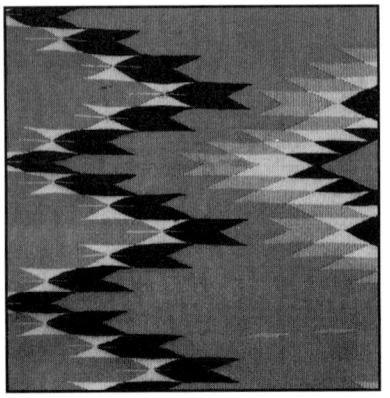

DETAIL

THE USE of the hourglass and chevron "chain" refers back to Saltillo-inspired designs.

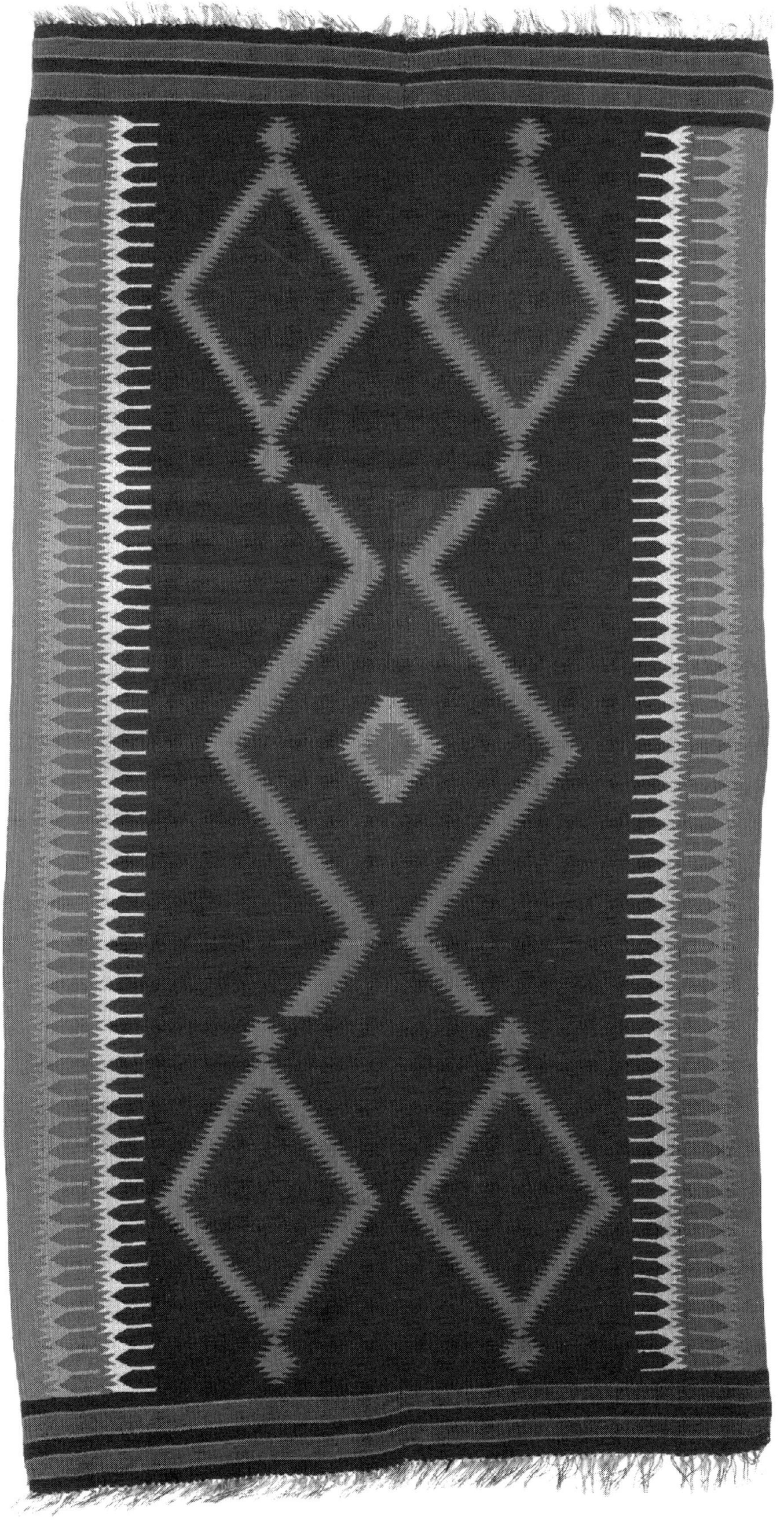

BLANKET 26

DESIGN SYSTEM:
Modern Chimayo Furniture or Floor Throw.

DIMENSIONS:
1.85 x .92 m. (6'1" x 3').
Fringe: 5 cm. (2").

PROBABLE DATE:
Ca. 1910-1930.

FABRIC STRUCTURE:
Weft-faced tapestry weave;
double width, center dovetailed seam.

FIBER:
Warp: 4-ply commercial cotton twine.
Weft: 3-ply synthetic-dyed Clasgens wool.

THREAD COUNT:
4:14/cm. (10:32/in.).

COLOR:
Black, blue, red, green, yellow, white.

DESIGN MOTIF:
Small serrate diamond center on a blue
and black even striped background with superimposed
green diamonds outlined in serrate red. Vertical selvage
border composed of vertical rows of *palmitas*.
Horizontal selvage bands of narrow stripes.

CONDITION:
Excellent.

COMPARABLE EXAMPLES:
Compare with the Ganado blanket (ca. 1900) in Plate
293, *Weaving of the Southwest*, p. 141. Also compare
the arrangement of the diamonds with
that of the Vallero eight-point star in Fig. 1,
Spanish Textile Tradition, p. 126.

COMMENTS:
The mixing of numerous textile influences and sources, what Cerny and Mather refer to as "Pan-Southwestern," affected all aspects of early twentieth-century weaving in New Mexico. This throw is an excellent example of that mixing. Woven on a Spanish horizontal loom, its pattern incorporates Navajo and Vallero-like motifs set against a Moki-inspired background.[141]

THE BACKGROUND PATTERN of even, repetitive stripes is derived from the "Moki" blanket, a pattern of regular stripes found in Hopi textiles.

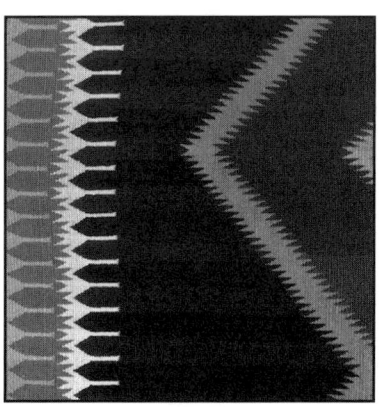

DETAIL

BLANKET 27

DESIGN SYSTEM:
Revival Striped Blanket.

DIMENSIONS:
2.28 x 1.43 m. (7'5½" x 4'8¼").
Fringe: None.

PROBABLE DATE:
Ca. 1930s.

FABRIC STRUCTURE:
Balanced plain weave;
single width, double-weave.

FIBER:
Warp: 4-ply commercial cotton twine.
Weft: 1-ply Z-spun handspun angora.

THREAD COUNT:
2-3:7/cm. (6:16/in.).

COLOR:
Red, green, orange, purple.

DESIGN MOTIF:
Symmetrical variegated stripes.

CONDITION:
Excellent.

COMPARABLE EXAMPLES:
None.

COMMENTS:
Jaramillo-Lavadie suggested that this blanket of pure angora weft is an example of the WPA weaving program established in New Mexico in the 1930s.[142] This blanket is the only example of near-balanced plain weave in the collection. In a true balanced plain weave, "warp and weft are equal in size spacing and count."[143] In this blanket, however, the weft is slightly thicker than the warp, yet the warp remains visible. Its surface texture is basket-like in appearance.

DETAIL

THE BASKET-LIKE texture of this blanket was achieved through the use of a near-balanced plain weave technique.

APPENDIX A

Comparative Materials

BLANKET 28
Classic Rio Grande Five-Band Blanket
Plate 5,
Spanish Textile Tradition, p. 61

BLANKET 29
Saltillo *Sarape*
Plate 17,
Spanish Textile Tradition, p. 77.

Reproduced with permission from Nora Fisher, Curator of Textiles, Museum of International Folk Art, Santa Fe.

APPENDIX A

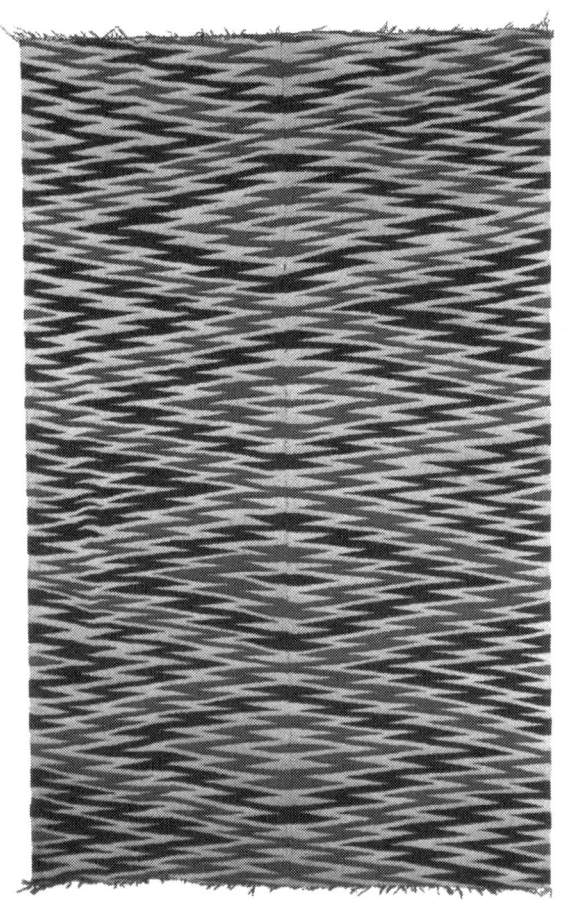

BLANKET 30
Rio Grande Saltillo-Style Blanket
(without border)
Plate 31,
Spanish Textile Tradition, p. 101.

BLANKET 31
Rio Grande Saltillo-Style Blanket
(with selvage bands)
Plate 34,
Spanish Textile Tradition, p. 103.

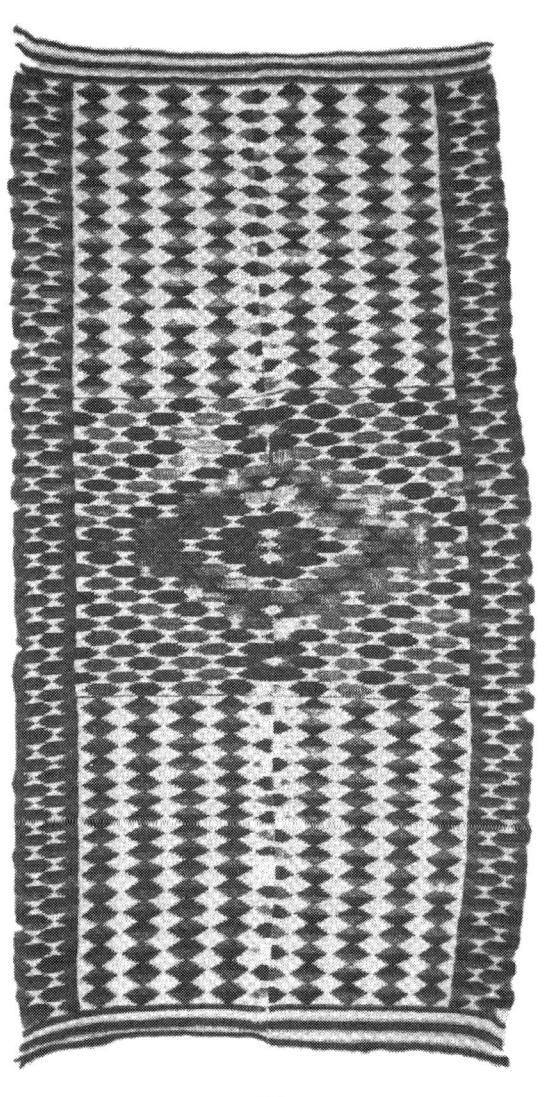

BLANKET 32
Rio Grande Saltillo-Style Blanket
(with frame)
Plate 39,
Spanish Textile Tradition, p. 109.

BLANKET 33
Rio Grande Seven-Band Blanket
with Saltillo Design Elements
Fig. 5,
Spanish Textile Tradition, p. 93.

APPENDIX B

Color Frequency Chart

THIS COLOR FREQUENCY CHART was developed to establish the frequency order of colors indentified in the blankets of the collection. Because of the disproportionate number of Transitional Period band and/or stripe blankets the collection (blankets 2 through 19), only these were recorded in the chart. The methodology used to prepare the chart was as follows:

FIRST, all colors found in the eighteen blankets were listed to the left of the chart, beginning with neutrals followed by colors in prismatic order.

SECOND, no more than seven colors were identified in any particular blanket, indicated by "primary" through "septenary" frequencies in the upper section of the chart.

THIRD, the number of times a particular color appears in the blankets was recorded in order of frequency in the chart itself. For example, the color "natural white" occurred as the primary color in ten blankets, noted as the first entry in the chart. When all of the numbers listed for a particular frequency are compared, color predominance can be established. To illustrate, a review of the data listed for the primary frequency indicates that natural white is the predominant color found in this sampling: it appeared as the primary color in ten of the eighteen blankets charted. Natural brown appeared as the primary color in only three blankets, etc.

FOURTH, the number of times a particular color appeared in all frequency positions was recorded in the extreme right column. Natural white was the color used most often in all frequency positions. Natural brown was the second most recorded color, followed closely by pink.

AND FINALLY, frequency numbers were totaled on the bottom row. These indicated the number of blankets which contained specific numbers of colors. All blankets boasted at least two different colors, while almost 90% contained three. 84.2% contained four colors, while fewer than 50% had five colors. Slightly more than 10% contained six colors, while only one blanket, or 5%, had seven.

Because over 84% of the blankets in the collection contained at least four individual colors of yarn, it was also possible to establish the order of predominance, or color choice, for these four colors. This is summarized on the following page.

Therefore, though the color palette expanded greatly in the Transitional Period, the weaver continued to select natural, undyed yarns as the primary weaving material, a tradition continued from classic blanketry.[144] Other colors most frequently selected, pink, purple, blue and green, relate in their prismatic placement to natural dyes found in classic blanketry, which included both dark and medium blue indigo and blue-red *cochineal*.[145] Perhaps things had not really changed as drastically as some authors have inferred.

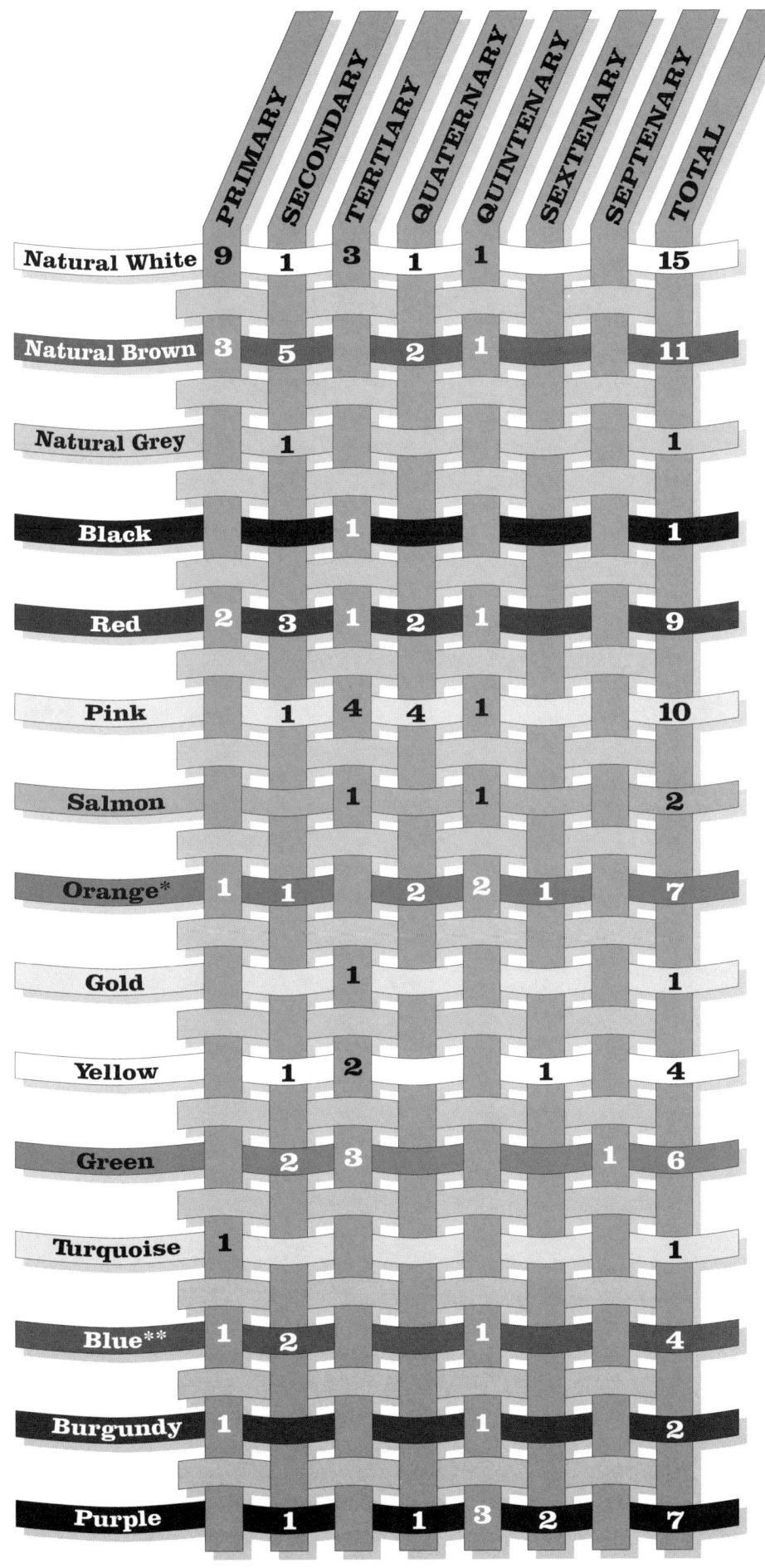

ENDNOTES

1 The twenty-seven blankets in this study are from the textile collection of Mr. Will and the late Mrs. Liz Doty of Norman, Oklahoma. They graciously allowed full access to their beautiful collection.

2 Dr. H.P. Mera finally wrote about the Rio Grande blanket in his ca. 1948 manuscript, unpublished until 1987. See Kate Peck Kent, ed., *Spanish-American Blanketry: Its Relationship to Aboriginal Weaving in the Southwest*, by H. P. Mera (Santa Fe: School of American Research (SAR), 1987).

3 Nora Fisher, ed., *Spanish Textile Tradition of New Mexico and Colorado* (*STT*) (Santa Fe: Museum of International Folk Art (MOIFA), 1979).

4 Many good publications exist on the Anasazi of New Mexico. A colorful publication is that by William M. Ferguson and Arthur H. Rohn, *Anasazi Ruins of the Southwest in Color* (Albuquerque: University of New Mexico (UNM) Press, 1988).

5 For a discussion of pre-conquest Spanish weaving see *Rugs of Spain and Morocco* by Florence Lewis May (Chicago: University of Chicago Press, 1977). The guild system and the *obrajes* of Colonial Mexico are described briefly by Suzanne Baizerman, "Textiles, Traditions, and Tourist Art: Hispanic Weaving in Northern New Mexico," (Ph.D. University of Minnesota 1987), p. 40. Baizerman's "Textile Examination Record" (Appendix C) was used as a model for the catalogue format in this text.

6 George P. Hammond and Agapito Rey, *The Rediscovery of New Mexico*, Coronado Cuatro Centennial Publication, 1540-1940, Vol. 3 (Albuquerque: UNM Press, 1953), p. 85. Cotton was domesticated by the Anasazi, the probable ancestors of the Pueblo, as early as A.D. 750, Ferguson and Rohn, p. 22. Though cotton fields were not recorded as being observed around the Rio Grande Pueblos, they were, according to Ward Alan Minge, "noted in the more temperate lowlands of New Mexico, and cotton cloth was found in great quantity among the Hopis," *Efectos del País:* A History of Weaving Along the Rio Grande," in *STT*, p. 10. And as noted by Antonio de Espejo in 1581, "the Indians spin cotton and weave cloth," *ibid*.

7 Minge, p. 9.

8 *Ibid*.

9 See Marc Simmons and Gene Turley, *Southwestern Colonial Ironwork* (Santa Fe: Museum of New Mexico (MNM) Press, 1980) p. 29.

10 Minge, p. 10.

11 *Ibid*., p. 11. And Joe Ben Wheat, "Rio Grande, Pueblo, and Navajo Weavers: Cross-Cultural Influence," in *STT*, p. 29.

12 France V. Scholes, "Church and State in New Mexico, 1610-1650: Chapter 5: The Administration of Luis de Rosas, 1637-1641," in *New Mexico Historical Review* (*NMHR*), 11, No. 4 (Oct. 1936), 307.

13 Scholes, *Troublous Times in New Mexico*, 1659-1670 (Albuquerque: UNM Press, 1942), p. 34.

14 Dorothy Boyd Bowen, "A Brief History of Spanish Textile Production in the Southwest," in *STT*, p. 5.

15 Kent describes the differences between the indigenous wide vertical (upright) loom and the Spanish horizontal loom: "Pueblos and Navajos wove single-width blankets on the indigenous vertical loom, the warp sets controlled by a string-loop heddle and a shed rod [shuttle] that were manipulated by hand, and the weft beaten down on the flat treadle loom of European derivation. Heddles were hung from above and were controlled by foot treadles, freeing the hands to manipulate the weft. Warps were passed between the dents of a reed, which spaced them and was used to beat the weft into place," "Spanish, Navajo or Pueblo?: A Guide to the Identification of Nineteenth-Century Southwestern Textiles," in *Hispanic Arts and Ethnohistory*, edited by Marta Weigel, et al (Santa Fe: Ancient City Press, 1983), p. 143. A heddle is "one of the sets of parallel cords or wires that compose the harness used to control warp threads on a loom." A reed is "a device on a loom resembling a comb and used to space warp yarns evenly." "Glossary," in *STT*, pp. 250-51.

16 Minge, p. 14.

17 *Ibid*.

18 Bowen, "A Brief History," p. 6. In the Rio Arriba, however, only two weavers and one Comanche carder were listed in the 1790 census, and both of these lived in Santa Fe. Weaving here lagged far behind that in the Rio Abajo, *ibid*.

19 See Wheat, "Rio Grande, Pueblo, and Navajo Weavers," p. 30. All Rio Grande, Navajo and Pueblo striped blankets are weft-faced plain weave. According to Irene Emery, "plain weave is the simplest possible interlacing of warp [vertical stationary yarns] and weft [horizontal manipulated yarns] elements . . . When the wefts are sufficiently numerous and sufficiently compacted to completely cover the warps, the fabric is weft-faced," *The Primary Structures of Fabrics* (Washington: The Textile Museum, 1966), p. 17.

20 Minge, p. 15.

21 *Ibid*. Eighteenth-century annual trade fairs were established at Saltillo, Mexico (September); Chihuahua, Mexico (July); San Juan de los Lagos, Mexico (December); and Taos, New Mexico (autumn). Bowen, "A Brief History," p. 6.

22 Minge, p. 15.

23 Bowen, "A Brief History," p. 6.

24 Wheat, "Spanish-American and Navajo Weaving, 1600 to Now," "Collected Papers in Honor of Margery Ferguson Lambert". In *Papers of the Archaeological Society of New Mexico*, 3 (1976), p. 200. Chacón's list echoes that compiled from wills and inventories of the eighteenth century.

25 Lansing B. Bloom, "Early Weaving in New Mexico," *NMHR*, 2, No. 3 (July 1927), 237.

26 Bowen, "A Brief History," p. 6.

27 Originally translated and annotated by H. Bailey Carroll and J. Villasana Haggard, *Three New Mexican Chronicles: The "Exposición" of Don Pedro Bautista Pino, 1812* . . . (Albuquerque, The Quivira Society, 1943), pp. 35-36. Minge offers a slightly different translation, p. 22.

28 Wheat, "Saltillo *Sarapes* of Mexico," in *STT* p. 74.

29 *Ibid*., p. 75.

30 Wheat, "Early Trade and Commerce in Southwestern Textiles Before the Curio Shop" (MS Santa Fe, MOIFA (1987?)), p. 17. Intermittent clandestine trade with the United States, especially through the intermediary French trader, had been going on for decades. Minge writes: "Trade with foreigners was incidental, though the French tried to establish connections with Santa Fe from the Mississippi prior to the French and Indian War in 1763. Contacts with the French in 1723 resulted in some exchange of clothing and bayeta . . . . The French continued a steady trade with the Plains Indians, the Comanches serving as agent to the Spanish colonists," p. 14.

31 Josiah Gregg, *Commerce of the Prairies*, ed. Max L. Moorehead, (1954; rpt. Norman: University of Oklahoma Press, 1954), p. 150. Gregg also notes the use of the *sarape* as "portieries, or couch-covers, where they do not get rough usage," p. 171.

32 Susan Shelby Magoffin, *Down the Santa Fe Trail and Into Mexico: The Diary of Susan Shelby Magoffin, 1846-1847*, ed. Stella M. Drumm

(New Haven: Yale University Press, 1926), p. 150. Magoffin also describes the use of *jerga* as floor covering, p. 154. Rio Grande blankets were also used as bed coverings, see the interior photograph dated 1888 by Charles Fletcher Lummis in *Chas F. Lummis—The Centennial Exhibition Commemorating His Tramp Across the Continent*, ed. Daniela P. Meneta (Los Angeles: Southwest Museum, 1985), p. 61.

33 Bowen, "A Brief History," p. 7.

34 Fisher and Wheat, "The Materials of Southwestern Weaving," in *STT*, p. 200.

35 *Ibid.*, and Baizerman, p. 57. Also see Alvar Ward Carlson, "New Mexico's Sheep Industry, 1850-1900: Its Role in the Territory," in *NMHR*, 44, No. 1 (Jan 1969), 80-83.

36 Bowen, "A Brief History," p. 7.

37 Bowen, "Introductory Remarks," in *STT*, p. 54. In a ca. 1880-82 photograph, a Saltillo-style Rio Grande blanket is used as a lap robe, *ibid.*, Fig. 1. p. 55.

38 Wheat, "Early Trade and Commerce," p. 19.

39 Baizerman, p. 47.

40 Wheat, "Early Trade and Commerce," p. 20. He suggests that perhaps as many as 35,000 blankets were actually purchased, *ibid*. Baizerman describes Indians depicted in paintings from the Bosque Redondo (1863/4-1868) as wearing "plain white [blankets] or blankets with simple striping, likely government issue Hispano blankets," p. 48 and Fig. 7. She also notes that New Mexican blankets "appeared in Cloud Shield's winter count, 1858-59. These blankets were bought by the Dakota's from [the trader] John Richards, who brought them from New Mexico, *ibid.*, and Fig. 6b.

41 Wheat, "Early Trade and Commerce," p. 21. As defined by Fisher and Wheat, the thread count indicates "a specific number of warps and wefts within a given unit," or a warp to weft ratio, "Materials," in *STT*, p. 196-97. "The early Rio Grande blankets generally have a warp count of five to seven and weft count of twenty-five to fify per 2.5 cm. (one inch). The later blankets which contain commercial cotton warps and lumpy wool wefts have a thread count range of six to eleven warps and thirty to forty wefts per 2.5 cm. (one inch)," *ibid*. The late blankets woven for the military were loosely woven and of extremely poor quality.
Furthermore, almost all handspun yarn in the Southwest was Z-spun, meaning that the direction of the spin in the yarn resembled the letter "Z," p. 197. Spin increases the strength of the yarn. These military blankets woven of unspun yarn would not have been durable.

42 Richard E. Ahlborn and Harry R. Rubenstein, "Smithsonian *Santos*: Collecting and the Collection," in *Hispanic Arts*, p. 241. The *bultos* (carved devotional images) of San Miguel and San Rafael by Captain Miera y Pacheco, a Spanish-born cartographer and artist residing in New Mexico in the third quarter of the eighteenth century, are displayed among Hispanic and Indian artifacts collected at Zuni by an early American ethnographer for the Smithsonian, *ibid.*, Fig. 1, p. 240, and cat. #s 1 and 2, pp. 244-45.

43 Bertha P. Dutton, "Commerce of the New Frontier: The Fred Harvey Company . . . ," in *Colonial Frontiers: Art and Life in Spanish New Mexico: The Fred Harvey Collection*, ed. Christine Mather (Santa Fe: Ancient City Press, 1983), Figs. 110, 112, pp. 94, 96. Unfortunately, Schwitzer kept less than adequate records of his purchases.

44 Charlene Cerny and Mather, "Textile Production in Twentieth-Century New Mexico," in *STT* p. 170. This fusion of Hispanic and Indian design has been labeled "Pan-Southwest" by the authors, who describe this phenomenon as "a mixture of motifs that bring to mind things both Indian and Spanish and carry a visual message of being simply southwestern," *ibid*.

45 Yvonne Lange, "Foreword," in *STT*, p. x.

46 *Ibid*. Mera's study of the late 1940s is basic to any study of Hispanic textiles, Kent (1987).

47 Lange, p. ix.

48 For a discussion of the Panama-Pacific Exposition, consult *Creator of the Santa Fe Style: Isaac Hamilton Rapp, Architect*, by Carl D. Sheppard (Albuquerque: UNM Press, 1988), especially Chapter VI, "Santa Fe Style," pp. 73-100.

49 *Ibid*. The first public expression in New Mexico of pueblo style architecture was that at the University of New Mexico (1904-1909) under President William George Tight. See John L. Kessell, *The Missions of New Mexico Since 1776* (Albuquerque: UNM Press, 1980), pp. 24-28. On the influence of the Santa Fe Style on furniture and interiors, see *New Mexican Furniture, 1600-1940* by Lonn Taylor and Dessa Bokides (Santa Fe: MNM Press, 1987), ch. III, pp. 213-40, especially the photographs on pp. 220-23. An interesting recollection of life in Santa Fe in the 1920s is that by Ruth Laughlin, "Santa Fe in the Twenties," *New Mexico Quarterly Review*, 19 (1949), 58-66.

50 Weigle, "The First Twenty-Five Years of the Spanish Colonial Arts Society," in *Hispanic Arts*, pp. 182-83; and Cerny and Mather, pp. 178-79. Mary Austin and Frank Applegate were major collectors of Hispanic art beginning in the seond decade of this century.

51 *Ibid*.

52 *Ibid*. For a detailed discussion of the Native Market, see Sarah Nestor, *The Native Market of the Spanish New Mexican Craftsmen: Santa Fe, 1933-1940* (Santa Fe: The Colonial New Mexico Historical Foundation, 1978).

53 Helen R. Lucero, "Hispanic Weavers of North Central New Mexico: Social/Historical and Educational Dimensions of a Continuing Artistic Tradition" (Ph.D. UNM 1986), p. 74.

54 Cerny and Mather, p. 180.

55 *Ibid*.

56 Baizerman, p. 108.

57 Weigle, ed. *Hispanic Villages of Northern New Mexico* (1935, rpt. Santa Fe: The Lightning Tree, 1975). Reprint of the original Tewa Basin Study with supplementary materials.

58 Lucero, p. 74.

59 Claudia Larcombe, "E. Boyd: A Biographical Sketch," in *Hispanic Arts*, p. 5.

60 *Ibid.*, p. 6.

61 Boyd, *Saints and Saint Makers of New Mexico* (Santa Fe: Laboratory of Anthropology, 1946), p. xx.

62 Kent, *Spanish-American Blanketry*, p. 11. Every subsequent publication on Rio Grande blankets credits Mera's manuscript as the foundation for the inquiry. See, for example, Lange, p. x.

63 Ina Sizer Cassidy, various articles in *New Mexico Magazine* (Sept. 1940 - Jan. 1955). For a complete listing, see *STT*, p. 257.

64 William H. Dusenberg, "Woolen Manufacture in New Spain," *The Americas*, 4, No. 2 (Oct. 1947), 223-34.

65 Catherine Drew Jenkins, *An Analysis of the Saltillo Style in Mexican "Sarapes"* (Berkeley: University of California, 1951).

66 Martha Tilley, *Three Textile Traditions: Pueblo, Navajo, and Rio Grande* (Colorado Springs: The Taylor Museum, 1967).

67 On the influence of the Spanish Colonial Arts Society, see Ann Vedder, "History of the Spanish Colonial Arts Society, 1951-1981," in *Hispanic Arts*, pp. 219-27.

68 Boyd, *Popular Arts of Spanish New Mexico* (Santa Fe: MNM Press, 1974).

69 William Wroth, ed., *Hispanic Crafts of the Southwest* (Colorado Springs: The Taylor Museum, 1977).

70 Juanita Jaramillo-Lavadie, "Rio Grande Weaving: A Continuing Tradition," in *Hispanic Crafts*, pp. 9-23.

71 Thomas J. Steele, S.J. *"Santos" and Saints: Essays and Handbook*

(Albuquerque: Calvin Horn Publisher, 1974); reprinted and updated as *"Santos" and Saints: The Religious Folk Art of New Mexico* (Santa Fe: Ancient City Press, 1982). The trend toward contextualization surfaced in the previous decade, but Steele's book had much greater impact. See George Mills, *The People of the Saints* (Colorado Springs: The Taylor Museum, n.d. (1967)).

72 Marta Weigle, *Hispanic Villages of Northern New Mexico* (Santa Fe: The Lightning Tree, 1975).

73 J. J. Brody, *Between Traditions: Navajo Weaving Toward the End of the Nineteenth Century* (Iowa City: University of Iowa Museum of Art, 1976); Mary Hunt Kahlenberg and Anthony Berlant, *The Navajo Blanket* (New York: Praeger Publishers, 1972*;* and Marian Rodee, *Southwestern Weaving* (Albuquerque: UNM Press, 1977).

74 Jean M. Burroughs, "From Coronado's *Churros*," *El Palacio*, 83, No. 1 (1977), 9-13; R.A. Donkin, "Spanish Red: An Ethnographical Study of *Cochineal* Red and the Opuntia Cactus," in *Transactions of the American Philosophical Society*, 67, part 5 (1977), n.p.; and J. Ehly, "Truchas Becomes a Weaving Center," *Handweaver and Craftsman*, 24, No. 4 (July/August 1973), 40.

75 Marianne L. Stoller, "A Study of Nineteenth-Century Hispanic Arts and Crafts in the American Southwest: Appearances and Processes" (Ph.D. University of Pennsylvania 1979); and Wheat, "Spanish Weaving Terms Used in the Documents" (MS Santa Fe, MOIFA 1977).

76 Cerny and Mather referred to late nineteenth-century textiles in passing. They characterized these as inferior to the textile production of "the period between 1820 and 1880 [which] represents the pinnacle of artistic achievement for the Spanish in New Mexico," p. 170.

77 Kent, "Spanish, Navajo, or Pueblo?" pp. 135-70.

78 Wheat, "Early Trade and Commerce," n.p.

79 Jaramillo-Lavadie, "1980-1981 NEA Folk Art Grant for the Study of Rio Grande Hispanic Textiles," Grant No. 10-5531-136 (MS Santa Fe, MOIFA (1982?); and Maria Vergara Wilson, "Spanish Colonial Textile Techniques" (MS Santa Fe, MOIFA 1982).

80 Lucero and Baizermans's joint publication is planned by UNM Press.

81 The permanent Spanish heritage exhibition, titled *Familia y Fe*, was co-curated by Wroth and Lucero, assisted by Robin Farwell, Curator of Spanish Colonial Collections. The exhibition opened in July 1989.

82 See Baizerman, pp. 170-77. She provides an excellent detailed analysis of transitional period blanket characteristics. Her model was used as the primary basis for the discussion in this chapter. The only apparent weakness in her analysis is the lack of visual comparative material.

Twenty-three of the twenty-seven blankets in this collection date from about 1880-1900. Twenty-one of these may be classified as transitional period blankets. Baizerman describes these as blankets produced from 1860-1910, woven of both handspun and commercial yarns dyed with either natural or synthetic dyes. Two of the twenty-four are Early Chimayo blankets. The Early Chimayo period dates from between 1880-1920 and overlaps the transitional period in time. Also in the collection are one example each of classic striped and Modern Chimayo and two examples of revival.

Because transitional examples are dominant in the collection, the focus of this chapter is the transitional period Rio Grande blanket. Characteristics of the period are defined in terms of changes in material, color and design, evaluated against characteristics associated with classic period blanketry. Dating of the blankets in this collection was established through design and material analyses as set forth in the book *Spanish Textile Tradition*.

83 Edward Norris Wentworth, *America's Sheep Trails* (Ames: Iowa State College Press, 1948), pp. 237-38. This citation is mentioned in every subsequent reference to the introduction of the Rambouillet-Merino in New Mexico. For example, see Bowen, "A Brief History," p. 7; and Stoller, "Spanish-Americans, Their Servants and Sheep: A Culture History of Weaving in Southern Colorado," in *STT*, p. 51. Also see Carlson, "New Mexico's Sheep Industry," pp. 30-31. The Rambouillet-Merino will hereafter be referred to, in the tradition of the previous literature, simply as "Merino."

84 Descriptions of the properties and characteristics of Merino versus *churro* may be found in both Stoller, "Spanish-Americans," p. 52, and Baizerman, p. 57.

85 Lucero notes that the *churro* was crossed with the Merino late in the nineteenth century in an effort of "upgrade" local stock, p. 148.

86 The most complete analysis to date on nineteenth-century dyes used by the Hispanic weaver is that by Spillman and Bowen, "Natural and Synthetic Dyes," in *STT*, Appendix D, pp. 207-11. Also consult Saltzman and Fisher, pp. 212-16.

87 None of the weavers and scholars who examined this blanket identified the red as *cochineal*. Most felt it was a synthetic color.

88 On natural dyes available in New Mexico, refer to Gail Tierny with Mary Klare, "Dye Plants Native to New Mexico, and Some Introduced Dye Plants that Have Been Cultivated There Since Spanish Colonial Times," in *STT*, Appendix F, pp. 217-20; Vergara Wilson; and Mela Sedillo-Brewster, "New Mexican Weaving and the Practical Vegetal Dyes from Spanish Colonial Times" (MA UNM 1935).

89 Spillman and Bowen, p. 210.

90 See the "Color Frequency Chart," Appendix B, this text.

91 Baizerman, p. 172.

92 Bowen, "Bands and Stripes with Saltillo Design Elements," in *STT*, pp. 83-99. Also called *manita*, "little hand," or *palma*, "palm." The motif in blanket 20 is unique in that it has an open beak-like end on an elongated stem. Usually the *palmita* has no stem, and ends in a simple point on one end. Compare with Fig. 1, Diagram, in *STT*, p. 84.

93 When shown blanket 22 independently, both Lucero and Vergara Wilson described it as a "blanket-within-a-blanket." Personal interviews conducted 15 Aug. and 13 July 1988, respectively.

94 For a brief description of commercial yarns, see Fisher and Wheat, p. 200. All information in this chapter on commercial yarns was adapted from this source.

95 *Ibid.*

96 David Ortega, personal interview, 13 Jan. 1989.

97 Fisher and Wheat, p. 199.

98 See Spillman, "Bands and Stripes," in *STT*, pp. 57-73; Bowen, "Bands and Stripes with Saltillo Design Elements," pp. 83-99; and Bowen, "Saltillo Design Systems," in *STT*, pp. 100-23.

99 Baizerman, p. 172.

100 Fisher, "*Vallero* Blankets," in *STT*, pp. 124-33.

101 See Baizerman, p. 172.

102 *Ibid.*, p. 67. Also consult Lucero, p. 35.

103 Kent, "Spanish, Navajo, or Pueblo?" p. 164.

104 Irene Emery, *Primary Structures*, p. 156.

105 Kent, "Spanish, Navajo, or Pueblo?" p. 164.

106 Fisher postulates that the wide reed began to be imported from the United States after 1880. No documented proof has as yet come to light, "The Treadle Loom," in *STT*, p. 195. Rodee notes that the wide loom was introduced to Chimayo by J. S. Candelario after 1890, *Weaving of the Southwest* (Albuquerque: UNM Press, 1987), p. 39.

107 Kent, "Spanish, Navajo, or Pueblo?" p. 164.

108 See Cerny and Mather, pp. 173-75.

109 In this indentification the term "blanket" is specifically applied. It does not appear that any of the textiles in this collection were originally intended as *sarapes*. None of the textiles contains a center repaired area that might have been used as a head slit.

110 Emery, p. 76.

111 *Ibid.*

112 *Ibid.*, p. 7.

113 "Glossary," in *STT*, p. 251. The authors prefer the spelling "selvadge." However, in *The New Lexicon Webster's Dictionary of the English Language* (New York: Lexicon Pub., Inc., 1988), the spelling "selvage" is preferred, p. 906. "Selvage" is used in the body of this text.

114 *Ibid.*

115 Emery, p. 11

116 When the fringe ends are "worked up" into the blanket, this means that they are finger-woven back into the body of the blanket.

117 See blanket 3.

118 Spillman, "Bands and Stripes," in *STT*, Fig. 2c, p. 59. A "shot" is a single pass of weft.

119 Spillman, "Bands and Stripes," Fig. 2a, p. 59.

120 Photographs of the interior of her home portray Dietrich as an avid collector of New Mexicana. Magretta Stewart Dietrich, *New Mexico Recollections*, Part II (Santa Fe: Vergara Printing Co., 1961), pp. 3-17.

121 Weigle, "The First Twenty-Five Years," p. 183.

122 Spillman, "Bands and Stripes," p. 62.

123 Fisher and Wheat, p. 199.

124 Jaramillo-Lavadie, personal interview, 14 July 1988.

125 On the issue of gender, Stolier says, "... shearing the sheep, initial cleaning of the wool, and carding were tasks generally performed by men as was building the looms. Hand spinning and dying the wool were usually the work of women (including women Indian servants) and children. Women were also more likely to attend to the of collection plants for the preparation of vegetal dyes. The actual weaving was done by both sexes. In sum, it took the work of both to produce textiles, but the tasks were not mutually exclusive. Men could spin - and some excelled in the craft - while women could also card, and it was not unknown for a woman to shear sheep." "The Hispanic Women Artists of New Mexico: Past and Present," *El Palacio*, 92, #1 (Summer/Fall 1986), p. 21. In the modern revival period, after about 1970, most Hispanic weavers in New Mexico are women. For example, the twenty-five weavers currently working at Tierra Wools, a Hispanic weaving cooperative in Los Ojos, New Mexico, are all women. Sophie Chávez, production manager for Tierra Wools, noted that there were two or three male apprentices in the early 1980s, but none have remained with the cooperative, and none, to her knowledge, continue to weave. Sophie Chávez, personal interview, 12 Dec. 1991.

126 Little has been written on the utility or camp blanket although these were probably the type most frequently woven in New Mexico. Few extant examples have been identified, perhaps due to the excessive wear they would have received. See Spillman, "Bands and Stripes," pp. 70-71.

127 *Ibid.*, p. 39

128 Jaramillo-Lavadie, personal interview, 14 July, 1988.

129 Allen Fannin, *Handspinning: Art and Technique* (New York: Van Nostrand Reinhold Co., 1970), p. 20. Felting indicates the ability of a fiber to matte itself. The more felting property possessed by a fiber, the easier it is to handspin.

130 Hammond and Rey, *Don Juan de Oñate, Colonizer of New Mexico 1591-1628*, Coronado Cuatro Centennial Publications, 1540-1940, Vol. 5 (Albuquerque: UNM Press, 1953), pp. 43-44.

131 E. A. Kay, "Perceptions of Three Cultures—Traditions Within the Chimayo Valley" (MA UNM 1985).

132 Fisher, "Fabric Structure," in *STT*, Fig 11, p. 205.

133 Jaramillo-Lavadie, personal interview, 14 July 1988.

134 *Ibid.*

135 Vergara Wilson, "Spanish Colonial Textile Techniques" (MS Santa Fe, MOIFA 1982), dye recipes, n.p.

136 Jaramillo-Lavadie, personal inverview, 14 July 1988.

137 Vergara Wilson, personal interview, 13 July 1988.

138 Jaramillo-Lavadie, personal interview, 14 July 1988.

139 Cerny and Mather, p. 171.

140 David Ortega, personal interview, 13 Jan. 1989.

141 Fisher, "*Vallero* Blankets," pp. 124-132.

142 *Ibid.*, "Fabric Structure," Fig. 1, p. 202.

143 Emery, p. 85.

144 Bowen and Spillman, p. 207.

145 *Ibid.*

REFERENCES CITED

Ahlborn, Richard E., and Harry R. Rubenstein. "Smithsonian *Santos*: Collecting and the Collection." In *Hispanic Arts and Ethnohistory in the Southwest (Hispanic Arts)*. Ed. Marta Weigle, et al. Santa Fe: Ancient City Press, 1983, pp. 241-82.

Baizerman, Suzanne. "Textiles, Traditions, and Tourist Art: Hispanic Weaving in Northern New Mexico." Ph.D. University of Minnesota 1987.

Bloom, Lansing B. "Early Weaving in New Mexico." *New Mexico Historical Review (NMHR)*, 2, No. 3 (July 1927), 228-38.

───────. "A Trade Invoice of 1638." *NMHR*, 10, No. 3 (July 1935), 242-47.

Bowen, Dorothy Boyd. "Bands and Stripes with Saltillo Design Elements." In *Spanish Textile Tradition of New Mexico and Colorado (STT)*. Ed. Nora Fisher. Santa Fe: Museum of International Folk Art (MOIFA), 1979, pp. 83-99.

───────. "A Brief History of Spanish Textile Production in the Southwest." In *STT*, pp. 5-7.

───────. "The Textiles: Introductory Remarks." In *STT*, pp. 54-56.

───────. "Saltillo Design Systems." In *STT*, pp. 100-23.

─────── and Trish Spillman. "Natural and Synthetic Dyes." In *STT*, Appendix D, pp. 207-11.

Boyd, E. *Popular Arts of Spanish New Mexico*. Santa Fe: Museum of New Mexico (MNM) Press, 1974.

───────. *Saints and Saint Makers of New Mexico*. Santa Fe: Laboratory of Anthropology, 1946.

Brody, J. J. *Between Traditions: Navajo Weaving Toward the End of the Nineteenth Century*. Iowa City: University of Iowa Museum of Art, 1976.

Burroughs, Jean M. "From Coronado's *Churros*." *El Palacio*, 83, No. 1 (1977), 9-13.

Carlson, Alvar Ward. "New Mexico's Sheep Industry, 1850-1900: Its Role in the History of the Territory." *NMHR*, 44, No. 1 (1969), 30-39.

Carrillo, Charles. Personal interview. 13 Jan. 1989.

Carroll, H. Bailey, and J. Villasana Haggard. *Three New Mexico Chronicles: The "Exposición" of Don Pedro Bautista Pino*. Albuquerque: The Quivira Society, 1943.

Cassidy, Ina Sizer. Various articles in *New Mexico Magazine* (Sept. 1940 - Jan. 1955).

Cerny, Charlene and Christine Mather. "Textile Production in Twentieth-Century New Mexico." In *STT*, pp. 168-91.

Chávez, Sophie. Personal interview. 12 Dec. 1991.

Dietrich, Margretta Stewart. *New Mexico Recollections*. Part II. Santa Fe: Vergara Printing Co., 1961.

Donkin, R. A. "Spanish Red: An Ethnogeographical Study of *Cochineal* Red and the Opuntia Cactus." *Transactions of the American Philosophical Society*, 67, part 5 (1977), n.p.

Dusenberg, William H. "Woolen Manufacture in New Spain." *The Americas*, 4, No. 2 (Oct. 1947), 223-34.

Dutton, Bertha P. "Commerce of the New Frontier: The Fred Harvey Company . . . " In *Colonial Frontiers: Art and Life in Spanish New Mexico*. Ed. Christine Mather. Santa Fe: Ancient City Press, 1983, pp. 91-104.

Ehly, J. "Truchas Becomes a Weaving Center." *Handweaver and Craftsman*, 24, No. 7 (July/Aug. 1973), 40.

Eldredge, Charles C., ed. *Art in New Mexico, 1900-1945: Paths to Taos and Santa Fe*. New York: Abbeville Press, Pub., 1986.

Emery, Irene. *The Primary Structures of Fabrics*. Washington: The Textile Museum, 1966.

Fannin, Allen. *Handspinning: Art and Technique*. New York: Van Nostrand Reinhold Co., 1970.

Ferguson, William M., and Arthur H. Rohn. *Anasazi Ruins of the Southwest in Color*. Albuquerque: University of New Mexico (UNM) Press, 1988.

Fisher, Nora, ed. *Spanish Textile Tradition of New Mexico and Colorado*. Santa Fe: MOIFA, 1979.

───────. "Fabric Structure ." In *STT*, Appendix C, pp. 201-06.

───────. "Introductory Remarks." In *STT*, Appendix E, p. 212.

───────. "The Treadle Loom." In *STT*, Appendix A, pp. 192-95.

───────. "Wef-Ikat Blankets." In *STT*, pp. 133-39.

───────. "*Vallero* Blankets." In *STT*, pp. 124-32.

───────, and Joe Ben Wheat. "The Materials of Southwestern Weaving." In *STT*, Appendix B, pp. 196-200.

"Glossary." In *STT*, pp. 151-52.

Gregg, Josiah. *Commerce of the Prairies*. Ed. Max L. Moorhead. 1950; rpt. Norman: University of Oklahoma Press, 1954.

Hammond, George P., and Agapito Rey. *The Rediscovery of New Mexico*. Coronado Cuatro Centennial Publications, 1540-1940. Vol. 3. Albuquerque: UNM Press, 1953.

───────. *Don Juan de Oñate, Colonizer of New Mexico, 1595-1628*. Coronado Cuatro Centennial Publications, 1540-1940. Vol. 5. Albuquerque: UNM Press, 1960.

James, George Wharton. *Indian Blankets and Their Makers*. Chicago: A. C. McClurg and Co., 1914.

Jaramillo-Lavadie, Juanita. "1980-81 NEA Folk Art Grant for the Study of Rio Grande Hispanic Textiles." Grant No. 10-5531-136. MS Santa Fe, MOIFA (1982?).

───────. "Rio Grande Weaving: A Continuing Tradition." In *Hispanic Crafts of the Southwest*. Ed. William Wroth. Colorado Springs: The Taylor Museum, 1977, pp. 9-23.

───────. Personal interview. 14 July 1988.

Jenkins, Katherine Drew. *An Analysis of the Saltillo Style in Mexican "Sarapes."* Berkeley: University of California, 1951.

Kahlenberg, Mary Hunt, and Anthony Berlant. *The Navajo Blanket*. New York: Praeger Publishers, 1972.

Kay, E. A. *Perceptions of Three Cultures—Traditions Within the Chimayo Valley*. MA UNM 1985.

Kent, Kate Peck, ed. *Spanish-American Blanketry: Its Relationship to Aboriginal Weaving in the Southwest, by H. P. Mera*. Santa Fe: School of American Research (SAR) Press, 1987.

———. "Spanish, Navajo, or Pueblo?: A Guide to the Identification of Nineteenth-Century Southwestern Textiles." In *Hispanic Arts*, pp. 135-70.

Kessell, John L. *The Missions of New Mexico Since 1776*. Albuquerque: UNM Press, 1980.

Lange, Yvonne. "Foreword." In *STT*, pp. ix-x.

Larcombe, Claudia. "E. Boyd: A Biographical Sketch." In *Hispanic Arts*, pp. 3-14.

Laughlin, Ruth. "Santa Fe in the Twenties." *New Mexico Quarterly Review*, 19 (1949), 58-66.

Lucero, Helen R. "Hispanic Weavers of North Central New Mexico: Social/Historical and Educational Dimensions of a Continuing Artistic Tradition." Ph.D. UNM 1986.

———. Personal interview. 15 Aug. 1988.

Luhan, Mabel Dodge. "The *Santos* of New Mexico." *The Arts*, 7, No. 3 (March 1925), 127.

Magoffin, Susan Shelby. *Down the Santa Fe Trail and Into Mexico: The Diary of Susan Shelby Magoffin, 1846-1847*. Ed. Stella M. Drumm. New Haven: Yale University Press, 1926.

Mather, Christine, ed. *Colonial Frontiers: Art and Life in Spanish New Mexico: The Fred Harvey Collection*. Santa Fe: Ancient City Press, 1983.

May, Florence Lewis. *Rugs of Spain and Morocco*. Chicago: University of Chicago Press, 1977.

McIntyre, Kellen Kee. "Transitional Period Rio Grande Weaving: Catalogue of the Will and Liz Doty Textile Collection." MA UNM 1990.

———, and Eric Lane. "Rio Grande Blankets." *New Mexico Magazine*, 70, No. 2 (Feb 1992), 50-57.

Meneta, Daniela P., ed. *Chas F. Lummis—The Centennial Exhibition Commemorating His Tramp Across the Continent*. Los Angeles: Southwest Museum, 1985.

Mills, George. *The People of the Saints*. Colorado Springs: The Taylor Museum, (1967).

Minge, Ward Alan. "*Efectos del País*: A History of Weaving Along the Rio Grande." In *STT*. pp. 8-28.

Nagen, Andrew, and Tyrone D. Campbell. "*Los Colores de Norte:*" *Rio Grande Weavings from the Ruth K. Belikove Collection*. Corrales, NM: Los Colores Museum, 1991.

Nestor, Sarah. *The Native Market of the Spanish New Mexican Craftsmen: Santa Fe, 1933-1940*. Santa Fe: The Colonial New Mexico Historical Foundation, 1978.

Ortega, David. Personal interview. 13 Jan. 1989.

Rodee, Marian. *Weaving of the Southwest*. Albuquerque: UNM Press, 1987.

———. *Southwestern Weaving*. Albuquerque: UNM Press, 1977.

Salzman, Max. "The Dye Analysis." In *STT*, pp. 214-216.

Scholes, France V. "Church and State in New Mexico, 1610-1650: Chapter 5: The Administration of Luis de Rosas, 1637-1641." In *NMHR*, 11, No. 4 (Oct. 1936), 297-333.

———. *Troublous Times in New Mexico, 1659-1670*. Albuquerque: UNM Press, 1942.

Sedillo-Brewster, Mela. "New Mexican Weaving and the Practical Vegetal Dyes from Spanish Colonial Times." MA UNM, 1935.

Sheppard, Carl D. *Creator of the Santa Fe Style: Isaac Hamilton Rapp, Architect*. Albuquerque: UNM Press, 1988.

Simmons, Marc, and Gene Turley. *Southwestern Colonial Ironwork: The Blacksmithing Tradition from Texas to California*. Santa Fe: MNM Press, 1980.

Spillman, Trish. "Bands and Stripes." In *STT*, pp. 57-73.

———, "*Jerga*." In STT, pp. 146-52.

———, and Bowen. "Natural and Synthetic Dyes." In *STT*, pp. 207-11.

Steele, Thomas J., S. J. "*Santos* and Saints: The Religious Folk Art of Hispanic New Mexico. Santa Fe: Ancient City Press, 1982.

———, "*Santos*" and Saints: Essays and Handbook. Albuquerque: Calvin Horn Publisher, 1974.

Stoller, Marianne L. "The Hispanic Women Artists of New Mexico: Present and Past." *El Palacio*, 92, no. 1 (Summer/Fall 1986), 21-25.

———. "A Study of Nineteenth-Century Hispanic Arts and Crafts in the American Southwest: Appearances and Processes." Ph.D. University of Pennsylvania 1979.

———. "Spanish-Americans, Their Servants and Sheep: A Culture History of Weaving in Southern Colorado." in *STT*, pp. 37-53.

Taylor, Lonn and Dessa Bokides. *New Mexican Furniture, 1600-1940*. Santa Fe: MNM Press, 1987.

Tierny, Gail, and Mary Klare. "Dye Plants Native to New Mexico, and Some Introduced Dye Plants that Have Been Cultivated Since Spanish Colonial Times." In *STT*, Appendix F, pp. 217-20.

Tilley, Martha. *Three Textile Traditions: Pueblo, Navajo, and Rio Grande*. Colorado Springs: Taylor Museum, 1967.

Vedder, Ann. "History of the Spanish Colonial Arts Society Inc., 1951-1981." In *Hispanic Arts*, pp. 205-18.

Vergara Wilson, Maria. "Spanish Colonial Textile Techniques." MS Santa Fe, MOIFA 1982.

———. Personal interview. 13 July 1988.

Weigle, Marta. "The First Twenty-Five Years of the Spanish Colonial Arts Society." In *Hispanic Arts*, pp. 181-204.

———, ed. *Hispanic Villages of Northern New Mexico*. Santa Fe: The Lightning Tree, 1975. (Rpt. of 1935 Tewa Basin Study with Supplementary Materials.)

———, ed, with Claudia and Samuel Larcombe. *Hispanic Arts and Ethnohistory in the Southwest*. Santa Fe: Ancient City Press, 1983.

Wentworth, Edward Norris. *America's Sheep Trails*. Ames: Iowa State College Press, 1948.

Wheat, Joe Ben. "Early Trade and Commerce in Southwestern Textiles Before the Curio Shop." MS Santa Fe, MOIFA (1987?).

———. "Rio Grande, Pueblo, and Navajo Weavers: Cross-Cultural Influence." in *STT*, pp. 29-36.

———. "Saltillo *Sarapes* of Mexico." In *STT*, pp. 74-82.

———. "Spanish Weaving Terms Used in the Documents," MS Santa Fe, MOIFA 1977.

———. "Spanish-American and Navajo Weaving, 1600 to Now." Collected Papers in Honor of Margery Ferguson Lambert. In *Papers of the Archaeological Society of New Mexico*, 3 (1976), pp. 199-226.

Wroth, William, ed. *Hispanic Crafts of the Southwest*. Colorado Springs: The Taylor Museum, 1977.

GLOSSARY

 Weaving terms and foreign words used in this text

aniline dye: Coal tar dye.
bayeta: Flannel.
botas: Man's leather leggings.
bulto: Carved devotional image.
bosque: Lowland woods along a river.
caballero: Gentleman horseman.
calzones: Trousers with a side slit decorated with silver buttons.
Camino Real: The Spanish royal trade route between Chihuahua and Santa Fe.
card: Tool used to disentangle and comb out fibers of wool, also the process of combing out fibers.
Chimayo: Center for production of Hispanic textiles for the tourist market, beginning in the last quarter of the nineteenth century, also the textiles produced there.
chaqueta: Embroidered, waist-length man's jacket.
charro: Upper class Spanish horseman.
churro: Common sheep of Spain. Introduced to New Mexico by Coronado.
cochineal: Red dye from dried and pulverized insect bodies.
colcha: Embroidered bed or altar covering. Also the particular embroidery stitch.
cortes: Spanish parliament.
efectos del país: Locally produced goods.
encomendero: Grantee of an *encomienda*.
encomienda: Grant giving grantee the right to collect tribute (dues or services) from the inhabitants of a designated area. It did not convey property rights.
entrada: Entrance of Spanish Conquistadors to an uncharted area.
frazada: Bedding blanket.
Germantown yarn: Commercially prepared yarn from mills in the region of Germantown, Pennsylvania.
grémio: Guild.
guía: Passport which frequently contains a cargo list.
indigo: Blue plant dye. Also anil.
harness: A device for raising and lowering warp threads on a loom. A loom can have two or more harnesses.
heddle: One of the sets of parallel cords or wires that compose the harness used to control warp threads on a loom.
jerga: Loom-woven floor covering or sacking.
kiva: Pueblo or Anasazi underground ceremonial chamber.
loom: A machine for weaving.
loom, treadle: A loom with beams which are used for storing long lengths of warp and cloth, and treadles (foot pedals) which control the warp threads. Brought to the Americas by the Spaniards.
loom, vertical, or upright: Indigenous American loom, best known example of which is the Navajo loom.
manita: Literally "little hand," a Saltillo design element.
manta: Variously defined as a woolen or cotton shawl, an Indian dress, a fabric commonly used as tribute, treadle-loom-woven commercial cloth, or unbleached sheeting.
Merino: Rambouillet-Merino sheep introduced to New Mexico in 1859 and bred with the *churro*.
"Moki": Old Spanish name for Hopi, a tribe of Pueblo Indians living in the northeast corner of present day Arizona. Refers to a particular Rio Grande pattern of alternating brown, indigo blue and white stripes.
mordant: Color fixer which combines with dyes on fibers to make them more permanent.
obraje: Weaving workshop.
ordenanzas: Spanish regulations affecting the output of the *grémios*.
palma: Literally "palm" or "hand," a Saltillo design element.
pueblo: Native town or village.
ply: One of the strands of a yarn. A 2-, 3- or 4-ply yarn consists of that many single elements twisted together.
ranchero: Owner of a modest rural property, or *rancho*.
reed: A device on a loom used to space warp yarns evenly. It resembles a comb.
Rio Abajo: Lower river, the area of the Rio Grande below the La Bajada Escarpment.
Rio Arriba: Upper river, the area of the Rio Grande above the La Bajada Escarpment.
sabanilla: Woolen sheeting.
Saltillo: Town in Mexico noted for its weaving.
santero: Maker of *santos*.
santo: Painted two-dimensional or sculpted devotional image.
sarape: Man's wearing blanket or poncho. Also serape, in English.
Saxony yarn: A fine, commercial 3-ply yarn.
sayal: Woolen cloth.
selvage: Woven edge of a fabric. Also selvadge.
shed: The passageway between the warp yarns through which the shuttle is thrown.
shuttle: A device on a loom for passing or shooting the weft thread through the shed from one side of the cloth to the other.
sombrero: Low wide-brimmed hat.
spinning: To make yarn by drawing out and twisting fibers into a continuous strand.
tapestry weave: Weft-faced plain weave fabric in which weft threads do not run from selvage to selvage but from isolated patterns or areas of color.
telar: Loom, treadle loom.
treadle: Foot pedal on a treadle or harness loom.
warp: Vertical stationary yarns on a loom.
weft: Horizontal manipulated yarns on a loom through the warp.
Vallero: Rio Grande blanket made in the El Valle area of New Mexico characterized by an 8-point star motif.
vara: Colonial measurement of length equal to about 33 in. or 84 cm.

ABBREVIATIONS

FAP - Federal Art Project
HABS - Historic American Building Survey
MA - Master's Thesis
MNM - Museum of New Mexico, Santa Fe, New Mexico
MOIFA - Museum of International Folk Art, Santa Fe, New Mexico
MS - Manuscript
NMHR - *New Mexico Historical Review*
Ph.D. - Dissertation
SAR - School of American Research, Santa Fe, New Mexico
STT - *Spanish Textile Tradition of New Mexico and Colorado*
UNM - University of New Mexico, Albuquerque, New Mexico
WPA - Works Projects Administration

INDEX

Angora goat, 16
Analine Dye, see coal tar dye, 21
Applegate, Frank, 25
Austin, Mary, 25
Bands and stripes, 21, 32, 34, 35
Bautista Pino, Don Pedro, 19
Bayeta, 18
Bazán brothers (Juan and Ignacio Ricardo), 19
Blanket-within-a-blanket, 34
Borders, 19, 20
Boyd, E., 30, 31
Burro Weavers, Santa Fe, 26
Camino Real, 19
Carding, 33
Cargo Lists, see Guías, 18
Casteñeda de Nájera, Pedro de, 16
Chacón, Governor, Fernando, 19
Chamuscado-Rodríguez expedition, 16
Chevron, 20
Chihuahua Fair, 19
Chimayo blankets, 11, 24, 35, 36
Churro sheep, 16, 21, 34
Clasgens yarn, 35
Classic Rio Grande blanket, defined, 35
Clothing: 16
Coal tar dye, 21
Cochineal, 34
Colonial Arts Shop, Santa Fe, 25
Cooke, George Brown, 23
Coronado, Francisco Vásquez de, 9, 16
Cotton, 16-19
Design motifs, 20
Design systems, 19
Dimensions, 36
Double-weave, 36
Double width, 36
Dovetailing, 36
Dyes, natural, 32, 34
Dyes, synthetic, 9, 34
El Paso Fair, 19
El Rito Normal School, 26
Encomienda, 17, 18
Fabric Structure, 36
Family weaving tradition, 9, 32, 36
Fewkes, Jesse Walter, 23
Frazadas, 18, 20, 21

Fred Harvey Company, 24
Gallegos, Hernán, 16
Germantown yarn, 21, 35
Gregg, Josiah, 20
Grémios, 19
Guías, 18
Indians, 20, 22-24
Indigo, 18, 34
James, George Wharton, 24
Jerga, 18, 20, 21
Land grants, 18
Looms, treadle, 16
Magoffin, Susan Shelby, 20
Manita, 20
Manta, 16-19
Martínez Baeza, Francisco, 17
McCrossen Handwoven Textiles, Santa Fe, 26
Meem, John Gaw, 25
Mendizabál, Governor, Bernardo Lopez de, 17
Mera, H.P., 9, 24, 30, 31
Merino sheep, see Rambouillet-Merino
Mexican independence, 20
Mission Style Revival architecture, 24, 25
Native Market, 25
Navajo, 7, 9, 18, 30, 31, 36
Obrajes (workshops), 16, 17, 20
Old Spanish Trail, 20
Oñate, Governor Juan de, 17
Ordenanzas (regulations), 19
Palma, 20
Panama-Pacific Exposition, San Francisco, 25
Pan-Southwestern motifs, 35
Perkin, William Henry, 21
Pino, Don Pedro Bautista, 19
Plain weave, 18
Pueblo Indians, 16, 18
Pueblo Revolt, 17
Railroad, 9, 21, 24, 36
Rambouillet-Merino sheep, 21, 33
Revilla Gigedo, Count, 18, 19
Rio Abajo, 9, 15, 18
Rio Grande blanket, defined, 9, 11, 24, 30, 32, 33, 36

Rosas, Governor Luis de, 17
Sabanilla (sheeting),18
Saltillo "leaf", 34
Saltillo *sarape*, 19, 20
San Luis Valley, 9, 15
Santa Fe Handwoven Textiles, Santa Fe, 26
Santa Fe Trail, 9
Santos, 23-25, 30
Sarape, 18-21
Saxony yarn, 21, 35
Sayal (sackcloth), 17
Schweitzer, Herman, 24
Selvage, 20
Sewell, Brice, 26
Sheep, 16-18
Smithsonian Institution, 24
Spanish Colonial Arts Society, 25
Spanish Market, the, 25
Spanish Pueblo Revival architecture, 24, 25
Spinning, 33
Stevenson, James and Matilda Coxe, 23
Stripes, see bands and stripes, 7
Tapestry weave, 34
Territorial Period, 21
Tewa Basin Report, 26, 331
Thread count, 21
Tlaxcala, 20
Tourist Art, 24
Trade, 20, 36
Trade Fairs, 23
Transitional Period Rio Grande
    blanket, defined, 33
Treadle loom, 16
Tribute, 17, 18
Úbeda, Fray Luis de, 17
Vallero blanket, 31, 36
Vargas, Governor Don Diego de, 18
Vertical loom, 16-18
Warp-weft ratios, 36
Wills and inventories, 18
Yarn, commercial, 9, 21, 35
Yarns, handspun, 17, 35

THIS BOOK was set in Century Schoolbook Roman and Italic and Clarendon Bold Extended. **GRAPHIC DESIGN** and pre-press production for this book was performed by John Pella and Greg Scott of Pella&Scott, Albuquerque, New Mexico. **THE HISTORIC MAP** was drawn in pen & ink by Moira North of Albuquerque. **ALL ORIGINAL** blanket photography was provided by Studio 7 / Albuquerque. **THE PRINTING** of this book took place at BookCrafters Publishing in Chelsea, Michigan.

THE MULTIPLE "Triple Stitch Pattern" devices seen repeatedly throughout the book are based on actual textile designs found in Transitional Period Rio Grande Blankets.

adobe gallery